Judging for Themselves

Learn how to use mock trials to bring history and literature to life! When students take on the roles of lawyers and witnesses in historical or literary trials, they develop greater investment in the topics, they learn rigorous close-reading and questioning techniques, and they are able to deeply explore and reflect upon themes of justice and responsibility. In this new book from award-winning teacher David Sherrin, you'll find out how this lively instructional strategy will make learning a more immersive, engaging, and memorable experience for your middle school and high school students. The book includes:

- a clear how-to guide to get the most out of mock trials in your class;
- ready-made units and lessons to get you started right away, complete with sample scripts, primary source documents, scaffolding worksheets, and assessment rubrics;
- templates and step-by-step instructions to help you design your own mock trials.

The pre-made units, which Sherrin spent years refining in his classroom, cover historical topics such as the Nuremberg Trials and the inquisitions of Martin Luther and Galileo. You'll also find fun and interactive mock trials based on the literary works *The Pearl* and *To Kill a Mockingbird*. These lessons will help students at all ability levels to become better readers, public speakers, and critical thinkers.

For even more engaging lessons, try out Sherrin's companion book on role-plays, *The Classes They Remember: Using Role-Plays to Bring Social Studies and English to Life*.

David Sherrin is an English and Social Studies teacher at Harvest Collegiate High School in New York City, where he is also the Social Studies Department Chair and the Master Teacher. At the 2014 NCSS Annual Conference, he was the recipient of the 2014 Robert H. Jackson Center National Award for Teaching Justice.

Other Eye On Education Books Available from Routledge
(www.routledge.com/eyeoneducation)

The Classes They Remember
Using Role-Plays to Bring Social Studies and English to Life
David Sherrin

Rigor in Your Classroom
A Toolkit for Teachers
Barbara R. Blackburn

Common Core in the Content Areas
Balancing Content and Literacy
Jessica Bennett

Teaching with Text-Based Questions
Helping Students Analyze Nonfiction and Visual Texts
Kevin Thomas Smith

Writing Behind Every Door
Teaching Common Core Writing in the Content Areas
Heather Wolpert-Gawron

DIY Project Based Learning for ELA and History
Heather Wolpert-Gawron

DIY Project Based Learning for Math and Science
Heather Wolpert-Gawron

Argue with Me
Argument as a Path to Developing Students' Thinking and Writing, 2nd Edition
Deanna Kuhn, Laura Hemberger, and Valerie Khait

Building a Community of Self-Motivated Learners
Strategies to Help Students Thrive in School and Beyond
Larry Ferlazzo

Create, Compose, Connect!
Reading, Writing, and Learning with Digital Tools
Jeremy Hyler and Troy Hicks

Math Lesson Starters for the Common Core, Grades 6–8
Activities Aligned to the Standards and Assessments
Paige Graiser

Teacher-Made Assessments
How to Connect Curriculum, Instruction, and Student Learning, 2nd Edition
Christopher Gareis and Leslie W. Grant

Judging for Themselves

Using Mock Trials to Bring Social Studies and English to Life

David Sherrin

Routledge
Taylor & Francis Group
NEW YORK AND LONDON

First published 2016
by Routledge
711 Third Avenue, New York, NY 10017

and by Routledge
2 Park Square, Milton Park, Abingdon, Oxon, OX14 4RN

Routledge is an imprint of the Taylor & Francis Group, an informa business

Library of Congress Cataloging-in-Publication Data
Names: Sherrin, David, author.
Title: Judging for themselves: using mock trials to bring social studies and English to life / by David Sherrin.
Description: New York: Routledge, 2016. | Includes bibliographical references.
Identifiers: LCCN 2015041202| ISBN 9781138644564 (hardback) | ISBN 9781138644571 (pbk.) | ISBN 9781315628745 (ebk)
Subjects: LCSH: Simulation games in education. | Social sciences —Study and teaching—Simulation methods. | English language—Study and teaching—Simulation methods. | Mock trials.
Classification: LCC LB1029.S53 S484 2016 | DDC 371.39/7—dc23
LC record available at http://lccn.loc.gov/2015041202

ISBN: 978-1-138-64456-4 (hbk)
ISBN: 978-1-138-64457-1 (pbk)
ISBN: 978-1-315-62874-5 (ebk)

Typeset in Optima
by Florence Production Ltd, Stoodleigh, Devon, UK

Printed and bound in the United States of America by Publishers Graphics, LLC on sustainably sourced paper.

To my grandparents—for your inspirational lives and the ways that your stories, choices, and values helped shape my own path.

Contents

Companion Website

Rubrics, video examples, templates, and reflection sheets for mock trials and role-plays can be found on David's website. Go to http://davidsherrin.wix.com/davidsherrin and click on the tab that says "Resources."

Meet the Author

David Sherrin teaches Social Studies and English at Harvest Collegiate in New York City, where he was a founding teacher and is the department chair. He is also the author of *The Classes They Remember: Using Role-Plays to Bring Social Studies and English to Life*. David's passion is to engage all students in learning about the complexities of the past through the use of role-playing, mock trials, and the analysis of primary sources.

David was named a New York City Master Teacher for 2014–2015 and was the recipient of the 2014 Robert H Jackson Center National Award for Teaching Justice. Previously, he taught at the Facing History School and at the Abraham Joshua Heschel School. David spent two years as a street educator for Projeto Axé, a Brazilian organization that provides education and outreach for street children in Salvador, Brazil.

David lives in Brooklyn with his wife, son, and dog. He enjoys cooking, eating well, reading about seventeenth-century Dutch history, and long subway commutes.

Acknowledgments

A successful mock trial is inevitably a work of collaboration and I have been the grateful recipient of the time and expertise of colleagues, friends, and family. First, I'd like to acknowledge the support of my principals, Kate Burch and Mike Dunson at Harvest Collegiate, and Gillian Smith, Dana Panagot, Mark Otto, and Kristina Wylie at Facing History, all of whom have encouraged my intellectual freedom in the classroom and the resulting development of mock trials for my students.

I have been fortunate to work alongside stellar teachers who not only have helped shape my thinking around curriculum and pedagogy but have also contributed their time during prep periods to work with my students on their cases and to accompany us to the courtroom for the trials. A special thanks goes out to Stephen Lazar and Andy del-Calvo for often lending an extra hand in these projects. Myles Brawer, my co-teacher for the past two years, has also been an invaluable support in working closely with students and providing key insights that hone our projects. A thank you to Andy Snyder is deserved for his constant counsel and friendly ear during the book-writing process and for his thoughtfulness about teaching students about the criminal justice system. I truly appreciate Joshua Vasquez, Jessica Jean-Marie, and Faye Colon for their work on developing a restorative justice practice at our school and for challenging me to expand my ideas on teaching about justice to include restorative models. Lastly, Nitzan Zir and Adam Sanchez have provided me with new avenues for exploring role-plays and mock trials and for thinking about their use in the classroom.

A number of friends have been invaluable partners in making my mock trials happen. John Schmidt, now a teacher at the Brooklyn Collaborative School, spent considerable time working in my classroom with struggling students as they were preparing for the trial. Adam Lubow, a public defender, has consistently made himself available to Skype with my students as they develop questions. He has also attended my trials to provide feedback to the students. Laureve Blackstone, an employment lawyer at Levy Ratner, has come to my class to work with students individually.

Vicky Vossen, a court attorney to a New York State Supreme Court Justice, was instrumental in setting me up in a courtroom as a mock trial venue for the first time, which was crucial in cultivating the aesthetic and visceral experience for my students.

A very special thanks goes out to the wonderful officers and staff, especially Chief Magliano and Captain Losi, at the Kings County Criminal Court who have always made our mock trial visits such a special occasion. I'm so grateful for the respect they have shown the students and their many efforts that have facilitated these memorable trips.

One of my nicest teaching moments comes when former students visit not only to say hi but to actually help my current students with their work. They serve as wonderful models for teenagers only a few years younger. I am so thankful to Shakina Kirton (who once served as lead prosecutor in my Rwanda Genocide trial) for returning years later to be a judge and to Bianca Serraty (a lawyer in my very first Galileo trial) for visiting my class nearly a decade later to help students with their preparation.

I'd like to make a special mention of appreciation for my father, Jeffrey Sherrin, the president of the law firm O'Connell and Aronowitz, who has answered my countless questions about the workings of the legal system, the intricacies of direct and cross-examination, and the nature of the trial system. He has also made himself available year after year for daytime conference calls to speak with students and provide them with guidance on questioning and opening and closing statements. It was certainly a measure of success when he attended a genocide mock trial and was blown away by the students' performances.

I have been fortunate to work with a wonderful team at Routledge where everyone is friendly, supportive, and outstanding at guiding me through the publishing process. My principle editor, Lauren Davis, has always been a thoughtful and calm partner in the work, even when unexpected pitfalls emerge that make us deviate from our plans. It is wonderful to feel that I not only have a brilliant editor looking at the book but also the guidance of someone who cares about what is good for me, for the book, and for the reading public.

It is not just a token gesture to thank my family. Education is deeply embedded in our hearts and many of our professional lives. I am certain that all that my mother and father taught me to value gets channeled into the work that I do with teenagers in the classroom. My sister, Nicki, and my brother-in-law, Matt, are both administrators and their stories are part of my educational conversation. My stepmother, Carol, began working as an inner-city teacher at about the same time I did, and we shared tales of success and failures.

My wife, Lea, has been a helpful listening partner since the start of my career. By now she knows well the ebbs and flows of the teaching calendar and the ways that my mindset begins to warp as mock trial courtroom days approach. I am especially thankful for her willingness to sit through my retellings of the trials and for making sure my shirt is tucked in on courtroom days.

Introduction

A Day in Court

> I think that being in an actual court house made the stakes higher which motivated me to spend more time preparing and think a little harder. There were times when I thought "alright, I'm done" and then I would think specifically about being in a court room and I would edit more and add more."
>
> (Oliver, 10th grader)

We are at a courthouse in Brooklyn for a mock Rwandan genocide trial of Athanese Seromba, a Catholic priest who allegedly participated in Hutu massacres of the Tutsi. The student playing a defense attorney strides to the podium to question the witness for the prosecution. They are both confident and prepared. "Isn't it true," she begins, "that you said you never saw Seromba at his house while the meeting was taking place?" He pauses. "Incorrect, he was there." She shuffles through papers, looking for the evidence. "That's not what you said in your affidavit," she retorts. The silence of the crowd transforms into oohs and claps, as if it were a sporting event. "You never saw Seromba with a gun, right?" she continues. "You never saw Seromba killing anyone?" The witness has no place to go. "No, I did not," he replies. "No further questions," the lawyer finishes, as she turns away.

Experiences like this one in the courtroom are some of the moments that I most look forward to during the school year and they are the ones in which I know that I've truly witnessed my students' learning. As I described in my previous book, *The Classes They Remember*, role-plays infuse much of my teaching and are at the heart of what I value and do in the classroom. Mock trials, while also a type of role-play, are a different element in my pedagogical table. They are much less kinesthetic/emotional, they don't involve imaginary swordfights or intrigue, and they are more traditionally cerebral.

My passion for mock trials, though, runs just as deep and I am as fully convinced of their effectiveness as tools for learning and assessments. As a mock trial day approaches I teach in top gear, filled with adrenaline and excitement, more than at any other point in the year. The reasons are multiple: students are performing and their knowledge is public; the outcome depends entirely on their work, but it is based on my effective preparation and scaffolding; students are taking on roles of historical or literary characters; outside partners, friends, and family are involved; and the students are engaging in some of the most challenging and multifaceted intellectual work that we can provide.

My experiences with mock trials began in my first year of teaching public school, when I created an early ancestor of my current Galileo and Martin Luther trials. We looked at primary sources together, I divided students into roles of various historical figures ranging from Pope Urban to Copernicus, and I watched gleefully as prosecuting lawyers pinned down witnesses with withering cross-examination questions.

Over the years, my mock trial repertoire and strategies developed far beyond that first attempt. I began emphasizing historical authenticity and the use of actual trial testimonies in my genocide tribunal trials for the Holocaust and Rwanda. As my teaching started to include a Humanities and English component, I created a mock trial for the famous case in *To Kill a Mockingbird* and also for imaginary literary trials, such as the one included for *The Pearl.* My mock trials have always been criminal trials; though my colleagues have shown me the value of civil ones as well.

Why Should We Do Mock Trials?

Here is why I do mock trials: they are challenging authentic projects in which students create and then do something "real." The projects serve as both learning and assessment tools since students learn from doing the work and teachers have a tangible product for evaluating understanding and growth. Mock trials are engaging for students and the role-playing aspect gets them out of their chairs, collaborating, and entering into the mindsets and perspectives of their characters.

Equally important, the preparation for the trials becomes what my colleague Steve Lazar called "one of the most rigorous projects I have ever seen students do." Why is that? First, the type of work is hard enough that law students take at least three years to master the art of legal questioning. More specifically, mock trials require students to read texts even more closely than normal in order to break them down, manipulate them, look for what *is and isn't* there, and then try to understand and use them to serve the goals of a particular character.

A mock trial is not just about getting students to answer questions. It is about having them figure out the answers to questions that you haven't asked and then getting them to write the questions for someone else to give those answers. It is about seeing evidence that is there but also about widening tiny gaps of what isn't there into gaping holes that, perhaps, makes a case burst open.

Mock trials are like role-plays with documents. Students recognize the challenging nature of the work. One 10th grader named Sophia wrote, "I felt like the mock trial was important because we worked so hard for all of us to get to that moment. The way of learning is really exciting and it gets me really interested in the topic that we are learning." Students need to see a text through the lens of their claims and perspectives. Bias and credibility are crucial concepts not only in the historian's work, but perhaps even more so in the eyes of a lawyer. In short, mock trials incorporate all of what great social studies teachers look for—claim, counterclaim, selection of evidence, use of evidence, perspective, and sourcing/bias–and puts it into a tantalizing package.

A strong mock trial cultivates the same level of student engagement as role-play, leading to high-quality work. One of my quietest students, Jonathan, wrote "The mock trial was like an experience of it actually happening. I think going into a courtroom and role-playing it is really fun because we don't just read and write we act; well, my favorite part out of the whole class was the courtroom. It helps learn in a living experience way."

Many people ask me the extent to which I delve into legal technicalities such as objections and introducing exhibits during these trials. For me, I keep in mind that I'm a social studies teacher using the legal structure as a tool for greater understanding and engagement as well as deep analysis of the text. I'm not teaching them legal procedure for its own sake. As such, I focus only on the core legal strategies for opening statements, closing statements, and questioning, which leads to rigorous thinking about claims, counterclaims, evidence, and sources. I do not feel it is necessary in the little time we have to go deeply into the nuance of procedure.

In *The Classes They Remember*, I provide a detailed explanation of the benefits of role-playing in general, whether in terms of the interactivity, the immersion, the cultivation of perspective and empathy, the analysis of choices, or the increase in student learning. Regarding learning, I refer both to the attainment and retention of knowledge/facts as well as a deeper understanding of the meaning of the content.

Mock trials lead to many of the same positive outcomes, especially when "game day" has the high stakes of taking place in a courtroom. The strategy also adds in a number of additional benefits: close-reading of texts, developing questioning techniques, and working as a team.

Before the day in court, mock trials are about intellectual preparation. The teachers are the cheerleaders, while the students are engaged in the heavy-duty intellectual work of the lawyer—reading carefully, crafting questions, thinking about holes in arguments, experimenting, and piecing together a case. When trial day comes around, they've finished the intellectual lifting and now need to put it in practice, in public, for all to see. It is a performance of their learning in the truest sense.

It is in this vein that I've become such a strong believer in this strategy—because it brings together the best of what we try to give students in their learning and in their assessments. I use mock trials as final assessments for a unit, but, unlike a test, it is a project in which *they learn* while we assess them.

There are a few elements that I particularly value in an assessment—that it reflects the learning and key ideas of a unit, that it allows students to grow in an important skill, and that it involves an authentic or "real" product that people produce in their jobs. Social Studies teachers often go the route of authenticity beyond the academic essay in terms of asking students to write a journalistic piece, design a cartoon, or produce a movie.

What is special about the "law" and the mock trial format? From my vantage point, it fully embodies all three of my major assessment goals. It is extremely rigorous in the close-reading of texts while also adding an additional factor: it is fun! The performance that takes place on courtroom day, including all the related pressures and foibles, adds an unforgettable texture to the experience for all involved. In short, a historical or literary mock trial is really enjoyable work that is really hard. Indeed, the nerves of trial day never completely outweigh the joy, the giggles, the shouts of encouragement, or the "ooohs" from the audience when a lawyer or witness hits a particularly strong point.

The rigorous nature of this strategy does not mean it is only for the elite. I have incorporated mock trials with diverse groups of students. I began them at Facing History School, a public high school in New York City that serves a high-needs population of students. I taught mainly 9th grade and developed mock trials to support students who were behind grade-level. My current school, Harvest Collegiate, serves a wider spectrum of the New York City population and the inherent differentiation within mock trial roles allows me to challenge the highest performers and to meet struggling students at their level. My students have varied from highly motivated achievers who end up at schools like Swarthmore (who love the trials) to students far behind grade-level with extremely low attendance (who also love the trials).

Given the advanced academic work involved in legal questioning, we might imagine that only the most highly skilled students can shine. This is not the case. First, the multiple avenues for differentiation (based on character roles) allows students to take on a task that meets their abilities and then to succeed at it. Second, the four or five days of preparation, and the chance to script out or practice questions and answers means that learners who need a little more time to "get it" can still achieve great success on the stand. Lastly, the performance aspect of the actual trial often brings out unexpected stars.

Teachers often talk about their "tool kit." I believe that this book can contribute a pretty solid hammer for any teacher to bring out at one or more points during a year. For me, not every unit is appropriate for an historical or literary trial, and we still need to dedicate time to traditional argumentative essays, research projects, literary analysis, and other assessments. Knowing its value, though, I try to engage my students in one to three trials during the year.

What Do We Mean by "Mock Trial"?

The term "mock trial" can take on various meanings. Most often, in schools, we use it to refer to a mock trial club in which students learn the intricacies of legal proceedings, including areas like the introduction of evidence and objections in order to take on a fictitious criminal or civil case and compete against other schools.

My strategy, which is meant to be used in the classroom, attempts to use the core of the legal format (witnesses, evidence, opening and closing statements, and direct and cross-examination questions) in order to build a realistic experience for students that develops important academic skills. For the most part, I am not concerned with the minutiae of trial rules unless they contribute to a key skill.

The Structure of this Book

Judging for Themselves provides the necessary guidelines and scaffolds for all teachers to be able to create their own mock trials and implement them in the classroom. It is based on nearly a decade of my own experimentation with the method and it includes my best trials, which you can just take and include in your curriculum.

The first two chapters provide my recipe for how to create and execute mock trials. I have made sure to include my most important worksheets and scaffolding tips, which I have revised year after year.

The following four chapters include my cornerstone trials, which could allow you to experiment with mock trials without having to simultaneously create a new one.

The first case involves Julius Streicher, a principal Nazi propagandist and one of the many defendants in the post-Holocaust Nuremberg Trials. The subject matter is intense and hopefully follows a deep exploration into the causes and atrocities of the Holocaust. Based on actual testimony and Streicher's writing, the case is powerful because of the ambiguities of responsibility, the issue of hate speech vs. freedom of speech, the power of words, the wealth of documentation, and the equilibrium of strength between the prosecution and the defense. The mock trial of Julius Streicher allows students to gain a deep understanding of the complexities of justice. As a propagandist, Streicher represented the moral ambiguities of responsibility. He killed no one and had few key roles in the Nazi government. But did his writings and drawings incite enough hatred towards Jews to make him responsible for the genocide? This chapter also provides all the relevant evidence documents.

The next chapter provides what can either be a combined inquisition trial of Martin Luther and Galileo, or two separate trials. Both individuals, of course, made historic challenges to the Catholic Church and as a result faced the risk of capital punishment for heresy. The trials use primary sources to juxtapose each man's thoughts and teachings with the doctrine of the Church. Students must make constant comparisons in order to elicit evidence that can demonstrate heresy or innocence. In this project, students learn to closely read primary sources and how to develop cross-examination questions that reveal perspective and bias. By performing an inquisition mock trial the students begin to question notions of justice and the impact of different types of justice systems. This section also includes all of the necessary witness documents.

The literary trials which follow take two forms, each of which is based entirely on the classic texts. *To Kill a Mockingbird* is a logical choice for a literary trial since the trial of Tom Robinson takes up such a significant portion of the book. In that chapter, I show how to modify the text in order to compose witness sheets (affidavits) that students can use as lawyers and defendants in the trial.

The following chapter enters into more creative territory by exploring how we can craft imaginary mock trials from works of literature, how we can use these trials to gain greater insights into characters and their motivations, and how we can further develop our students' close-reading skills. I use *The Pearl* as an example to flesh out this strategy and I provide the necessary information for English teachers to implement a trial of Kino or create their own with another piece of literature.

I'm hopeful that this book can lead to mock trials becoming a significant part of your teaching toolbox. I recommend that all readers carefully go through the chapters on creating and executing mock trials, and then pick and choose the sample projects that are relevant to their curriculum.

PART

1

A Mock Trial How-To Guide

CHAPTER 1

Creating Mock Trials

Figure 1.1 Students at the Julius Streicher Mock Trial

Creating a Mock Trial

Preparing a successful mock trial can be daunting. Over the past decade I've made mistakes that lower, a bit, the outcome for the students. Thankfully, I keep learning with each attempt and I think my current structure provides a deeper learning experience.

Here is a breakdown of the necessary steps for producing a new trial: choosing and teaching a story; selecting a defendant; choosing the witnesses; deciding where to hold the trial; organizing the logistics; putting together the assignment and scaffolding sheets; creating the affidavits and exhibits; determining the stipulated facts; and assigning the students.

Choosing and Teaching a Story

With myriad fascinating historical trials it might be difficult to choose one for the class if the goal is simply to do a mock trial. For me, however, mock trials came about when the actual historical trial was a key moment, or fulcrum, upon which a larger historical narrative turned. The trials in this book were each a central moment in a much larger chapter in human history, whether the Protestant Reformation, the Scientific Revolution, or the Holocaust. Given the demands of preparing and executing a mock trial, it makes more sense if the project fits into the larger content goals of your course. Only do a trial of Julius and Ethel Rosenberg if you're spending time looking at American reactions to the Cold War.

For the trial to have meaning it needs to come after learning about the larger event and the larger context of history. Before our Nuremberg trial we spend weeks learning about the causes of the Holocaust, Nazi policies, and the concentration camps. We also study Martin Luther and Galileo before our cases not only because it provides meaning for them, but also because they cannot actually do the trial without that base comprehension. Since we are using primary sources set in those times and places, there is too much complex vocabulary, whether about "indulgences" or the "Copernican System" that could trip students up, unless they already understand them. In short, choosing a trial case means fitting it within a larger historical unit for your course.

One common question about mock trials is whether to do a trial that actually happened or an imaginary one. I fall firmly in the former camp, although it is a bit more from a gut reaction than anything else. My sense is that since there is so much "history" out there for students to learn that *did* happen, it doesn't make much sense to spend time and effort engaging with something that *didn't*. By focusing on a trial that did happen we can then also have real discussions about its implications, consequences, and the perceptions around it. My goal is to make any role-play, even a trial, as authentic as possible and that can happen only through using actual witnesses and sources.

Selecting a Defendant

I made some errors in the past in choosing defendants and, thankfully, figured them out to the betterment of my subsequent trials. In some cases choosing the defendant is a self-evident step, such as in a trial of Martin Luther, Galileo, or *To Kill a Mockingbird.* When we're looking at a genocide trial, however, the number of possible defendants expands considerably. Years ago I made the mistake of putting a Rwandan army general on trial, and with his evident guilt the trial ended up too one-sided. It was still exciting and the kids learned an incredible amount. But it wasn't the right defendant to use.

I now make sure to have a defendant who brings out moral complexities, who could be reasonably found either guilty or not-guilty, and whose case matter is accessible to students. I considered a few possibilities for a Nuremberg trial. First I looked for a possible doctor who we could put on trial, perhaps one who had done experiments on Jews and abused his authority as a physician. This time, I ran into a new dilemma, which was that I could not locate enough primary source material to put together a great trial with authentic evidence about the doctor. I knew, moreover, that if I put someone like Eichmann, Hess, or Goering on the stand the defense would have a nearly impossible case (interestingly, the same year there was a major mock trial of Herman Goering at the national Model UN conference, which I thought was a mistaken choice given his obvious culpability).

I began to consider three different witnesses at the same time, all of whom were defendants in the principle Nuremberg trial: Walter Funk, Albert Speer, and Julius Streicher. Funk and Speer were industrialists and economists, which raised an interesting moral dilemma about responsibility. Were those who financed the war, the army, and the camps responsible for the genocide? Julius Streicher, meanwhile, was a propagandist who used his newspaper, *Der Stürmer,* as a launching pad to incite hatred of Jews.

To choose between these three defendants I dove into the testimony of their cases to get a sense of what type of evidence would be available for the students to read. Using the Yale Avalon website, which has translation of the original court transcripts, I pored over the transcripts of the trials to begin to separate out the statements of possible witnesses. I gathered evidence for about 15 witnesses for Streicher and about 13 possible witnesses for the Funk case. When I began to look deeper into Speer's case, I realized that the economic nature of his work was just not as comprehensible. I couldn't seem to glue together coherent statements that would make sense to my students. So, I threw him out of the running.

At that point I realized that I had a similar issue with Funk's testimony. Yes, there was enough of it, but the content was so highly economic and technical that my students would have an extra layer of difficulty to wade through without a strong economic vocabulary. There are enough other tough things for them to do in this project. It probably wouldn't be as interesting for them. In the case of Julius Streicher, on the other hand, the evidence was available and the theme, propaganda, was both accessible and highly interesting to them. The testimonies were at a reachable level and his case raised thought-provoking issues about culpability. By the time the concentration camps were underway, the Nazi Party had mostly exiled Streicher and he was living on a farm. He took part in no major decisions involving the Holocaust, except possibly on *Kristallnacht,* and he was not involved in the organization or running of the camps or the firing squads. For him, then, the main question is whether the words and images that appeared in *Der Stürmer* served as a direct cause of the genocide. What is the power of our words? He became the right defendant.

Choosing the Witnesses

Choosing the witnesses who will take the stand is another essential (and time-consuming) part of composing a trial. Having the right witnesses can make or break the success of a case.

My first rule of "witness selection" is to attempt to be as authentic as possible. Who was actually involved in the trial? When I first began my trials of Martin Luther and Galileo I stretched too wide and far in selecting witnesses. I chose people like Johannes Kepler and Erasmus who were involved in the wider discussions about Galileo and Luther but who played no role in their actual trials. I liked using them because they could discuss pieces of key evidence, like a letter that Galileo wrote to Kepler. But the students didn't learn how this trial really worked.

As I've leaned towards greater authenticity over the years, I first whittled the witnesses down to people who were directly involved in those cases like the pope or Cardinal Robert Bellarmine. Only more recently, however, did I realize that even this was not enough. These were not American trials with outside witnesses. They were inquisition cases with only one witness: the defendant. The attempt to hold an inquisition trial using the American criminal justice format was hindering student understanding of the event and the idea of justice. I realized that the only witnesses to use were the only two actual witnesses: the defendants Martin Luther and Galileo. Everything needed to be about how they saw and responded to key statements and writings by themselves and by authorities of the Church.

A literature trial like *To Kill a Mockingbird* does the work for us. The obvious witnesses to use are the ones that the author created for the trial, whether Tom Robinson or Maybelle Ewell.

A greater challenge is in putting together a full trial in the format of the American criminal justice system or an international genocide tribunal, whether we are talking about a case of the killers of Emmett Till, the Rosenberg trial, or Julius Streicher. Here, the first step is to understand who the witnesses actually were in the cases.

Figuring out how to gather enough witnesses for the defense and the prosecution in the Streicher case meant first reading through court records and testimonies on the Yale Avalon website. Some options were obvious: the people who were actually called to the stand like his wife, Adele Streicher, himself, Friedrich Strobel (a government official), and Fritz Herrwerth (his driver).

Needing more prosecution witnesses, I began to include people who spoke of Streicher in other texts, such as Victor Lutze, chief of the Nazi stormtroopers (SA). I made one of Streicher's illustrators into another witness. Each was there to comment on articles and drawings in *Der Stürmer*. Students had to try to understand the sources from these characters' perspectives and what they said about Streicher.

Now, however, I cleave even closer to the actual process. At Nuremberg, the prosecution made its case not by calling its own witnesses but instead by submitting the astounding number of self-incriminating documents that the Nazis had created. As you will see, in this project the only witnesses are defense witnesses, the actual ones who were called to the stand, and the prosecution must make its case through cross-examination and use of exhibits.

Deciding on a Venue

The classroom or an auditorium is always a venue option for a trial, especially if you spruce it up to mimic the intended atmosphere. In the inquisition trials, I have made poster-sized images of stained-glass windows and played Gregorian chants for sound effects. Think of how to best rearrange desks and chairs to replicate a courtroom.

The importance of a realistic venue in upping students' buy-in during the project comes out repeatedly in their reflections. Shona, one of Julius Streicher's defense attorneys, wrote: "Going to the courthouse made it seem that much more important to be prepared . . . actually being Streicher's lawyer made me more enthusiastic. I went home and kept on quoting the exhibits at home for my dad and how I thought in our case he shouldn't have been hanged." Oliver, who cross-examined Streicher, had the same realization: "I think that being in an actual court house made the stakes higher which motivated me to spend more time preparing and think a little harder."

Now I try to plan ahead and use my time to secure a better venue that will build excitement and authenticity, whether a church for the inquisition trials or a courtroom for others. It is necessary, of course, to obtain permission from officials at the courts beforehand to use them, but I have found local courthouses eager to open their doors for student mock trials. This requires advanced planning and careful calendaring, but the outcome of a "trip" trial is unbeatable.

Organizing the Logistics

There are certain pieces of the mock trial puzzle that you want to put in place early in the process, such as who you want present on the trial day and who you want to support students in their preparation. I've found such goodwill in the legal community and educational non-profits to partner in this work. Some potential helpers are lawyers, other teachers, parents, tutors, and former students. I try to find lawyers who can come in on days three or four of the preparation to provide one-on-one support. I also consider others who might join on the day of the trial as jury members.

Here's the thing: getting more hands on deck just takes foresight and planning, which are things I only occasionally have. Unfortunately, I often reach out to law firms and friends too late in the process. We all need some advanced notice to fit in volunteer work.

Keep in mind additional logistical requirements like permission slips and notifying your administration and other teachers of a trip. Remind students of the option to dress up for the trial and give examples of professional attire. It may seem like an afterthought, but if you're out of the building for a long chunk of the day don't forget to take into account food and lunch for students. Nothing will ruin a great educational experience like hunger!

Putting Together the Assignment and Scaffolding Sheets

My goal is to keep the assignment sheet brief to get the students working on the case immediately. In the next chapter I provide templates for instructions, for assigning student roles, and scaffolding sheets for developing questions and opening/closing statements.

Composing effective scaffolding sheets requires experimentation and practice. I modify them regularly depending on the type of trial. Given the complexity of question creation and the various factors in play, no scaffolding sheet can be perfect for all witnesses. Still, what is here are strong go-to templates. In the Nuremberg trial section, I've provided two types for direct and cross that you or students can choose from and that can be used for any trial. Consider filling out the scaffolding sheets yourself using the witness affidavits and exhibits to see how they pan out and to catch any snafus.

I find, however, that for students much of the work actually happens just using the sheets as a base and then working on them and around them, which is perfectly fine. The sheets are there if they need them.

Creating the Affidavits and the Exhibits

Creating the witness source documents is the hardest and most time-consuming part. Selecting the evidence students will use must be done purposefully. Of anything you produce for a trial, the students are going to spend the most time with the evidence or source documents so we need to make them thoughtfully and effectively. Consider issues such as length, complexity of vocabulary, and sophistication of the ideas. Think carefully about what the students can handle and what can challenge them.

One reason I love these trials is that students spend so much time dissecting one or two sources. Normally, we read something and move on. With trials, the evidence sheets may appear too hard at first glance. They probably are. Students often don't "get" their evidence sheets right away. This is the beauty of spending four days prepping for the trial, all of which, for each student, are spent on the same one to three pages of text. First, they struggle to understand it. Then, they strive to pull out ideas and evidence. Finally, they connect the dots, piece together a case, and write questions that support their positions.

My main rule for evidence sheets (affidavits + exhibits) is to be authentic. If there is testimony from the trial, adapt it into an affidavit. If the trial refers to the defendant's writings or other texts, use them as exhibits. You may create general exhibits that all lawyers and witnesses have access to or ones that are specific to certain witnesses and included alongside their affidavits.

To clarify, affidavits refer to sworn testimony taken before a trial. In my mock trials, I use "affidavit" to refer to an evidence sheet that includes the actual words of a particular witness, which I normally excerpt and adapt from real case testimony. Exhibits refer to additional documents or primary sources directly related to the case. For example, the evidence sheet for Adele Streicher (Julius's wife) includes her adapted testimony as an affidavit plus one of

Original Transcript	Adapted Transcript
DR. MARX: When did you become Herr Streicher's secretary and for how long were you in that job? FRAU STREICHER: On 7 June 1940, I became Julius Streicher's secretary and I remained in that job until the end of the war.	
DR. MARX: And during that period, you were continuously on his farm? FRAU STREICHER: Yes, I was always with him. DR. MARX: Were you also in charge of all the correspondence for Herr Streicher? FRAU STREICHER: Yes. DR. MARX: What did that correspondence mainly consist of? FRAU STREICHER: Mainly letters to his sons and to relatives. DR. MARX: What were Streicher's activities during that period of 5 years? FRAU STREICHER: Julius Streicher did mainly physical work; that is, agriculture and gardening, and from time to time he wrote articles for *Der Stürmer.*	On 7 June 1940, I became Julius Streicher's secretary and I remained in that job until the end of the war. I was always with him on the farm and I was in charge of his correspondence, which was mainly letters to his sons and to relatives. During that time, Julius Streicher did mainly physical work; that is, agriculture and gardening, and from time to time he wrote articles for *Der Stürmer.*
DR. MARX: During these 5 years did he leave the farm at all or was he ever absent from the farm for any length of time? FRAU STREICHER: During the first few years of his stay there Julius Streicher did not leave the farm at all; later, once in a while, he would pay a visit in the neighborhood. His longest absence did not comprise an entire day and never a single night.	During the first few years of his stay there Julius Streicher did not leave the farm at all; later, once in a while, he would pay a visit in the neighborhood. His longest absence did not comprise an entire day and never a single night.
DR. MARX: Did you know that it was prohibited for prominent Party members to visit Herr Streicher?	

Original Transcript	Adapted Transcript
FRAU STREICHER: Yes, there was such a prohibition. DR. MARX: How did you know that? FRAU STREICHER: From conversations. Then, too, I myself remember, when Dr. Goebbels visited the farm, that Julius Streicher said to him, "Doctor, you dare to come here? Do you not know that it is prohibited by the Party chiefs to visit me?" DR. MARX: When did the visits of Dr. Ley and Dr. Goebbels occur? FRAU STREICHER: Dr. Ley came to the farm on 7 May 1944. The visit of Dr. Goebbels occurred on 4 June 1944.	When Dr. Goebbels visited the farm, Julius Streicher said to him, "Doctor, you dare to come here? Do you not know that it is prohibited by the Party chiefs to visit me?" Dr. Ley came to the farm on 7 May 1944. The visit of Dr. Goebbels occurred on 4 June 1944.

Streicher's articles as an exhibit. The students playing the lawyers (whether prosecution or defense) questioning Ms. Streicher may use any of these documents to compose their questions. The student playing her as a witness also has access to them to prepare.

As mentioned above, the need to select, excerpt, adapt, and match up sources with witnesses means I spend considerable time compiling the evidence sheets.

I always "shop" first in the court record, whether the transcripts or a final judgment. In the Nuremberg case of Julius Streicher, I utilize the Yale University Avalon Project website, which provides the trial transcript. With it, I can compose affidavits for all of the defense witnesses. If we look below at a brief excerpt of Adele Streicher's testimony, though, we notice a few difficulties in using it. First, the text includes the questions of the lawyer, Dr. Marx. We want students creating the questions, so we need to get rid of them in an adapted version that becomes Ms. Streicher's affidavit. When we do so, however, the text no longer makes perfect sense because her statements are in the form of answers to questions that are no longer there. As a fix, I make minimal adaptations to maintain the integrity of the original.

We also need to take into account that lawyers enter into the record evidence as exhibits that doesn't come out in the transcript. At Nuremberg, the prosecution made its case against Streicher with copious examples of his speeches and articles from *Der Stürmer.* The students can't grasp the case or make cogent arguments without access to excerpts from *Der Stürmer* or his speeches. To provide this, I used Professor Randall Bytwerk's invaluable website of Nazi propaganda. I excerpted the texts for length and matched up each one with an affidavit on a related topic. For example, one defense witness in his affidavit might argue that Streicher never advocated violence against Jews. Hence, that witness' evidence sheet includes that statement plus an exhibit with one of Streicher's speeches in which he proposes extermination. This allows the prosecuting lawyer, doing cross-examination, to attack the claim from the affidavit by comparing it with the exhibit.

The key move, for me, is to identify a main topic or theme for each witness and then to ensure that the witness' evidence sheet includes two texts: one that (mostly) supports the defense and one that (mostly) supports the prosecution. Having contradictory texts side-by-side opens up a wealth of options for the lawyers on both sides to dig deeply in their questioning.

Every trial requires similar adaptations to provide what the students need and nothing they should not have—all in a manageable space.

For the inquisition trials, my method of composing the evidence sheets was entirely different. The trial transcript is a short one in which Galileo recants, which takes away the possibility for a student defendant, playing Galileo, to mount a real defense. So, unusually, I don't use that as a resource. I want to leave it up to the defendants how to "play" their characters. Consequently, I needed to find relevant primary sources and since the charge is heresy, I need to create a set of two competing sources for each witness: one from the defendant and one from the Church. This allows the prosecuting lawyers to identify contradictions between Galileo or Luther and the Church to make a case about heresy.

To do this, I identified ways in which each defendant might have gone against the Church. For Martin Luther, that could be through writing about indulgences, challenging the Pope's authority, providing an alternative view on salvation, or permitted marriage among clergy. I located a text from Luther that deals with one of those themes, like indulgences, and then I identified a Church text about the same issue from that time or prior to it. I have, for example, a sermon from Luther about indulgences competing against one by Johann Tetzel. I have Luther's 95 Theses about the pope's authority up against a 1302 Papal Bull by Pope Boniface VIII that deals with papal primacy. In this case, using a text by a previous pope works perfectly because a church lawyer could use such a document to demonstrate an established position of Church theology that Luther was contradicting.

Similarly, in the Galileo trial, the first witness receives two exhibits: one with biblical excerpts from Psalm 19 and Joshua 10 about the sun moving, and another from Galileo's *Dialogue Concerning the Two Chief World Systems* in which one of his characters declares "it is quite certain that not the earth, but the sun, is to be found at the center of the universe." All the witnesses have documents that provide this type of contrast, such as a letter from Cardinal Robert Bellarmine in which he states, "Council prohibits interpreting Scripture against the common consensus of the Holy Fathers" and a letter from Galileo in which he writes, "Given that in many places the Scripture is not only capable but actually needs interpretations different from the apparent meaning, it seems to me that in disputes about natural phenomena the Bible should be reserved to the last place."

Remember, it is valuable to take a few central sources and place them in the main instruction sheet as exhibits for all lawyers and witnesses to have access to them.

Assigning the Students

One compelling aspect of mock trials is that they inherently differentiate for widely diverse skill levels. We can thoughtfully assign different roles and texts to challenge each student at just the right level.

In my first trials, I made my four strongest students into the lawyers who were required to develop all of the questions, whether direct or cross-examination. All other students shared witness roles. I did this so that the highest skilled students could carry the most difficult task and receive a commensurate challenge while struggling students had easier roles.

My problem with this approach, now, is that the burden was too much on those four students and it did not allow any others to learn legal questioning strategies. I realized that more students could be lawyers by dividing up the witnesses and texts between them.

Currently, I tend to have different lawyers for each witness and I assign them based on the difficulty of each task/role. The hardest job, for my strongest students, is cross-examination because they're not necessarily writing questions about what is there. Instead, they must find holes, problems, bias, and contradictions.

The witnesses and the lawyers doing direct examination can collaborate together on the questions. My "middle" learners become witnesses and they can help create their own questions that they will answer on the stand. Being a witness requires the ability to think on one's feet and to process information quickly. My struggling students take on the role of lawyers doing direct examination, whether for the defense or the prosecution. Direct examination is easier and they have the support of the witnesses.

This system for mock trials has increased collaboration, provided opportunities for all, and targeted the needs of all students. It is authentic differentiation.

When I have more than one class doing the project, then I can increase the student engagement and the amount of scaffolding by having the classes compete against each other. One group becomes the defense and the other the prosecution. This allows more students to work together and it helps me focus each class on making the same case or argument. I can provide a little more direct instruction to the whole class if they are all doing the same work and on the same team.

Witness and Direct Examination Preparation Sheet (Option 1)

Direct examination: these are your witnesses. You need to ask open-ended questions (not "yes" or "no") to get them to tell a story. The witness and lawyer doing direct examination should work on this together using the text.

What is the witness' main claim and main supporting reason?

____

Table 1.1 Witness and Direct Examination Preparation Sheet (Option 1)

Clues	**Information to Help your Case (Quotation or Summary from Text)**	**Open-ended Question(s) to Ask for Witness to Discuss that Information**
Name of witness		
Witness' job; other key background information		
Witness' relationship to the defendant		
A key date(s)/event(s) in testimony? Witness' location at that date		
Reason/evidence #1 from text to support your case		
Reason/evidence #2 from text to support your case		
Reason/evidence #3 from text to support your case		
Reason/evidence #4 from text to support your case		
Reason/evidence #5 from text to support your case		

What is the main point that you want to make sure to clarify and repeat?

____

____

Witness and Direct Examination Preparation Sheet (Option 2)

Direct examination: these are your witnesses. You need to ask open-ended question (not "yes" or "no") to get them to tell a story. The witness and lawyer doing direct examination should work on this together using the text.

What is the witness' main claim and main supporting reason?

___

Table 1.2 Witness and Direct Examination Preparation Sheet (Option 2)

Clues	**Information to Help your Case (Quotation or Summary from Text)**	**Open-ended Question(s) to Ask for Witness to Discuss that Information**
Name of witness		
Witness' job; other key background information		
Witness' relationship to the defendant		
A key date(s)/event(s) in testimony? Witness' location at that date		
Major point of the story/testimony		
Major point of the story/testimony		
Major point of the story/testimony		
Major point of the story/testimony		

What is the main point that you want to make sure to clarify and repeat?

___

___

Cross-Examination Preparation Sheet (Option 1)

This is the other side's witness. You need to force the witness to make a mistake. *Find a hole in his/her story.* Find another way to see the text. You can lead the witness. *Ask only "yes" or "no" questions.* Make a statement that seems like a question. Find ways to *discredit* the witness by exposing bias or lack of information/knowledge.

What is the witness' main claim and main supporting reason that you want to make sure to address?

____

Table 1.3 Cross-Examination Preparation Sheet (Option 1)

Clues	**Information to Help your Case (Quotation or Summary from Text)**	**Yes/No Question(s) for Witness to Get Him/Her to Admit that Information**
Name of witness		
Witness' job; other key background information		
Witness' relationship to the defendant		
1 reason the witness lacks credibility (bias, etc.)		
2nd reason witness lacks credibility		
1 key piece of information the witness doesn't know or didn't see		
1 key piece of information that is vague or could be understood in a different way		
2nd key piece of information that is vague or could be understood in a different way		
1 inconsistency within text (witness says something contradictory)		
Statement(s) that contradicts key evidence from a defense exhibit		

Cross-Examination Preparation Sheet (Option 2)

This is the other side's witness. You need to force the witness to make a mistake. *Find a hole in his/her story.* Find another way to see the text. You can lead the witness. *Ask only "yes" or "no" questions.* Make a statement that seems like a question. Find ways to *discredit* the witness by exposing bias or lack of information/knowledge. Find the following in the text:

1. Lack of credibility (bias).
2. Misinformation.
3. Lack of information.
4. Vagueness.
5. Inconsistency/contradiction within itself.
6. Statement(s) that contradicts key evidence from an exhibit or stipulated fact.

What is the witness' main claim and main supporting reason that you want to make sure to address?

Table 1.4 Cross-Examination Preparation Sheet (Option 2)

Clues	**Information to Help your Case (Quotation or Summary from Text)**	**Yes/No Question(s) for Witness to Get Him/Her to Admit that Information**
Name of witness		
Witness' job; other key background information		
Witness' relationship to the defendant		
– Lack of credibility (bias) – Misinformation – Lack of information – Vagueness – Inconsistency – Contradicts an exhibit or fact		
– Lack of credibility (bias) – Misinformation – Lack of information – Vagueness – Inconsistency – Contradicts an exhibit or fact		
– Lack of credibility (bias) – Misinformation – Lack of information – Vagueness – Inconsistency – Contradicts an exhibit or fact		
– Lack of credibility (bias) – Misinformation Lack of information – Vagueness – Inconsistency – Contradicts an exhibit or fact		

Opening and Closing Statement Preparation Sheet

One or two lawyers on your team should write the statement.

Preparation before writing: Ask the lawyers and witnesses on your "team" about the most important point they will make. Write down one key point for each witness/lawyer.

Opening: Write a one-page statement outlining your side's case, highlighting the major points you will argue in the trial (you don't need to use actual quotations, just the most important broad points). Think of this as an introduction to your case. You will give this opening statement at the start of the trial.

Closing: Write a one-page statement outlining the case your side made, highlighting the major points you argued in the trial (you don't need to use actual quotations, just the most important broad points). You will give this closing statement at the end of the trial.
Here are some key things to think about:

1. What are the key values or issues that are at stake? What values of justice support your case? How would a victory for your side lead to justice?
2. Make sure to write in a clear, accessible tone. Write to the judges or jury and explain what you will show and they will see. You should have phrases like those listed in Table 1.5.

Table 1.5 Opening and Closing Statement Sentence Starters

Opening	Closing
• My team of lawyers will show . . . • Honorable judges, you will see that . . . • We will demonstrate that . . . • It will become clear during this trial that . . . • Once you see the evidence, you will recognize that . . . • Some of our witnesses will explain that . . .	• My team of lawyers showed that . . . • Honorable judges, you saw that . . . • We demonstrated that . . . • It became clear during this trial that . . . • With the evidence we saw, you should recognize that . . . • Our witness ________ showed that . . .

Jury/Judge Notetaking Sheet

Instructions: You are a member of the jury. You are here to judge the defendant's guilt or innocence. Remember you need to determine if there is enough evidence to convict the defendant *beyond a reasonable doubt.*

The Charge: ____

____

Name of Defendant: ______________________________

Table 1.6 Jury/Judge Notetaking Sheet

	Evidence that Shows Defendant is Guilty	**Evidence that Shows Defendant is Not Guilty**
Witness 1: Name:		
Witness 2: Name:		
Witness 3: Name:		
Witness 4: Name:		
Witness 5: Name:		
Witness 6: Name:		
Witness 7: Name:		
Witness 8: Name:		
Witness 9: Name:		
Witness 10: Name:		

Table 1.7 Additional Notes

Who was the key witness for you or what was a key piece of evidence?	Do you believe the defendant was guilty or not guilty?	If guilty, what do you think the punishment should be?

CHAPTER 2

Executing Mock Trials

Preparing Students for the Trial and Teaching the Skills

With careful planning, I can prepare students for a successful trial with four or five days of classwork. Here is how I break down the lessons for each day in their most basic form. In the following section I will use the Streicher trial as an example, but the strategies and steps hold true for any historical or literary trial.

Day 1: Preparation

The first day of trial preparation is about setting out the case and preparing students for the tough intellectual work that is coming. I have all the trial documents ready and when students walk in the door I immediately assign them their roles, point them to the materials, and have them sit with their partners. On the board, the warm-up says: "Find your role and evidence sheet, sit with your partner, read the project instructions."

We read the overview of the project together and I "sell" the trial with a statement or two like "this will certainly be a highlight of the year." One way that I motivate students to do the subsequent hard work is by showing a brief video-clip of a previous class' mock trial. We discuss what we see students doing in the clip. What type of work needs to be done to make this happen? If you don't have this available, you could always show a brief excerpt of a courtroom show or movie, such as *My Cousin Vinny* or *Law and Order*.

Now we need to delve into the details of the case itself. If students have already studied about the defendant, such as Galileo, then a biographical overview is unneeded. If not, we read a brief biography of the defendant, such as the United States Holocaust Museum website's overview of Julius Streicher. As we read, we look for initial clues for aspects of his life that could be reasons why he is on trial. For instance, we identify Streicher's role in organizing a boycott of Jewish stores and his ownership of an anti-Semitic newspaper.

The next step, which is crucial, is to read and clarify the indictment. What is the nature of the charge? In the Streicher trial, for example, he faces two main charges, each of which contain a number of examples. The charge of "Crimes against Humanity" includes acts such as deportation and persecution against a race or religion. As we read the indictment, we connect the charges back to the biography we just examined and try to preview the case. For instance, students might identify that Streicher's role in *Kristallnacht* could lead to support for an accusation of the "plunder of public and private property" within the indictment. This moment is about bringing out what we imagine are some of the fundamental points of the case.

If necessary, we take a few moments to explain the meaning of each role: witness, prosecuting attorney, and defense attorney. It is also important to clarify whether the whole class is working together (and in what role) or if different members of the class are competing against each other.

We close out the class by introducing students to their evidence sheets. I explain that in this first day of trial preparation, students should read through their evidence sheets (affidavits and exhibits) once or twice and mark down information that shows the defendant as either guilty or not guilty. The sheet has a visual code for not-guilty Δ and guilty Ψ I remind them that regardless of whether they are defense or prosecuting lawyers, they need to know the evidence that supports either position. Normally, students will only begin this process of reading the evidence.

I project the following instructions for the bulk of the period:

Trial Prep Instructions: Day 1	
1.	Make sure you know your roles, have your evidence sheet, and understand the project.
2.	Read your evidence sheet and code the evidence (guilty/not-guilty).

Most of this first day is spent in silent reading. I don't ask them to start writing questions yet. Day 1 is just to read the sources and begin to gather the evidence, which they should continue to do for homework.

What am I doing as students are reading? I know that the texts are difficult primary sources; I know that many students haven't fully grasped the instructions; I know that many students can only learn to do this by "doing" and not by hearing instructions, so I am mostly in triage mode. I'm circulating and giving a quick tip to various students, checking in on confusions in the reading, and guiding them toward key evidence. I assign the rest of their text for homework.

Day 2: Close Reading

Students do heavy-lifting on the second day of trial preparation. I know that some students still haven't fully gone through their texts. Most have not yet identified their key evidence. That is what this day is for.

When we begin, I make sure groups of lawyers working with particular witnesses are sitting together. The focus of the lesson is on close reading and annotation, which means looking for evidence of innocence and guilt. It is necessary to explain to the students that they are reading an affidavit from a witness testifying about the defendant. So they are not trying to find evidence about the witness' guilt, but rather about the defendant's.

It is important to note that none of the trials presented in this book are typical American criminal justice trials. In the inquisition trials, everyone is either a prosecutor doing cross-examination or a defendant. In the Streicher trial, since the only witnesses are for the defense, everyone is either a prosecutor doing cross-examination or the defense doing direct. This simplifies matters a bit in the teaching. In an American trial, however, since there are witnesses for both the prosecution and defense, then both sides have lawyers doing cross and others doing direct examination. This complicates a bit any effort in doing full-class modeling and I suggest, instead, to call over smaller groups to go over the different type of work they will be doing.

I begin by projecting an excerpt of the instructions at the top of every evidence sheet. This allows me to point out the symbols for identifying evidence of guilt or innocence.

Witness for the Defense 1: Fritz Herrwerth
Directions: Read the affidavit of Fritz Herrwerth, driver of Julius Streicher. Note any evidence that could be used to show he is innocent of crimes against humanity with Δ. Note any evidence that could show he is guilty with Ψ. Write 5–10 questions for this witness.

Witness for the Defense 2: Adele Streicher

Key Idea: Streicher's role in Nazi policies from 1941-45.

Witness:
Defense Lawyer (Direct):
Prosecuting Lawyer (Cross:

Directions: Read the following affidavit of Adele Streicher, wife to Julius Streicher. Note any evidence that could be used to show he is innocent of crimes against humanity with **Δ.** Note any evidence that could show he is guilty with **Ψ.**

Lawyers and Witness: Write 5-10 questions for this witness

Adele Streicher Affidavit[1]

On 7 June 1940, I became Julius Streicher's secretary and I remained in that job until the end of the war.

During that time, Julius Streicher did mainly physical work; that is, agriculture and gardening, Δ and from time to time he wrote articles for *Der Stuermer.*

During the first few years of his stay there Julius Streicher did not leave the farm at all; later, once in a while, he would pay a visit in the neighborhood. His longest absence did not comprise an entire day and never a single night. Δ Ψ

When Dr. Goebbels[2] visited the farm, Julius Streicher said to him, "Doctor, you dare to come here? Do you not know that it is prohibited by the Party chiefs to visit me?"

Dr. Ley came to the farm on 7 May 1944. The visit of Dr. Goebbels occurred on 4 June 1944.

Both visits were of a rather unofficial character. Dr. Ley wanted mainly to know how Julius Streicher was doing, personally. No political questions were raised. Ley said only, "Streicher, the Fuehrer is waiting for you." Ψ

Julius Streicher answered that he had become accustomed to his solitude, that he was happy as a farmer, and that Ley should tell the Fuehrer that he, Streicher, wanted nothing more. At the visit of Dr. Goebbels the subject of the conversation dealt mainly with Julius Streicher's dismissal from his office as Gauleiter, and Dr. Goebbels was of the opinion that Julius Streicher should return into the circle of old Party members; but he gave him the same answer, "Tell the Fuehrer I wish for nothing." Δ

[1] http://avalon.law.yale.edu/imt/04-29-46.asp#fraustreicher

[2] Joseph Goebbels was a German politician and Reich Minister of Propaganda in Nazi Germany from 1933 to 1945. As one of Adolf Hitler's closest associates and most devout followers, he was known for his zealous orations and deep and virulent antisemitism, which led him to support the extermination of the Jews and to be in strong support of the Final Solution.

Isn't it true that...
...., right?
...., correct?

Figure 2.1 Stephanie's Annotation for Streicher Trial

I then show a short excerpt of the affidavit so I can model how to mark it up.

> I was employed on 15 October 1934, in Nuremberg, not in the personal service of Herr[1] Streicher himself, but in the municipal motor pool. However, I worked for the then *Gauleiter*[2] Streicher.
>
> When Herr Streicher went to bed, I was usually with him or the house superintendent. On that evening, November 9, 1938, Herr Streicher went to bed earlier than usual.

I explain that students should spend half the period just reading the affidavit and/or exhibits, and annotating the texts with those symbols. It is crucial that students understand that they must look for evidence on both sides: their ability to win depends on them seeing and countering the opposing side's argument. Notice in Stephanie's annotation, in figure 2.1, how she identifies evidence that supports either side, regardless of her particular role. A particularly strong move that she makes is to select one sentence and use both codes, meaning that both the prosecution and the defense could capitalize on it.

Table 2.1 Sample Close Reading Scaffolding

Clues	**Information to Help your Case (Quotation or Summary from Text)**	**Open-ended Question(s) to Ask for Witness to Discuss that Information**
Name of witness	Fritz Herrwerth	
Witness' job; other key background information	Motorist	
Witness' relationship to the defendant	Worked as a driver for Streicher	
A key date(s)/event(s) in testimony? Witness' location at that date	November 9, 1938 – *Kristallnacht*	
Reason/evidence #1 from text to support your case	Streicher went to bed early that night	

Table 2.2 Close Reading: Looking for Bias or Vagueness

Clues	**Information to Help your Case (Quotation or Summary from Text)**	**Yes/no Question(s) for Witness to Get Him/Her to Admit that Information**
Name of witness	Fritz Herrwerth	
Witness' job; other key background information	Driver	
Witness' relationship to the defendant	Streicher's driver	
Lack of credibility (bias) – Misinformation – Lack of information – Vagueness – Inconsistency – Contradicts an exhibit or fact	As his driver, they talked a lot, perhaps were friends	
Lack of credibility (bias) – Misinformation – Lack of information – Vagueness – Inconsistency – Contradicts an exhibit or fact	"Herr Streicher went to bed earlier than usual" What time? Why?	

I also show them a short "clip" of the scaffolding sheet and how to transfer key information from the evidence sheets onto the chart. I model this at the beginning, but explain that they should spend the first half of the class only reading, and in the second half of the class they can begin filling out the worksheet. I tell them to just fill out the left-hand column.

It is necessary to point those students doing cross-examination in a bit of a different direction. Their first read of the document should be the same as above: a basic annotation for evidence of guilt and innocence. Their second read, however, is a bit more complicated. Whereas direct examination can focus on finding evidence to support their case, cross-examination needs to mostly find weaknesses in the other side's witness. To do this, I begin to direct them toward one strategy for each time they read it.

So, to model their second read, I focus them on bias. I model filling out the chart for Herrwerth's left-hand column and we highlight the bias, which is in this case that they were friends.

Then I model how we can search for a lack of information or vagueness that we can exploit. We need to find something that is not so clear, which could leave room for interpretation. Maybe the fact that he went to bed earlier than usual meant he didn't know about *Kristallnacht,* but maybe it could mean something else.

Students spend the rest of the period working on reading the documents, identifying evidence, and filling out the chart's left-hand column (information).

Most of the students on Day 2 will not be ready to write questions yet. During the latter part of the period, however, some will be at that point. Here, I think it is best to meet with them individually, when necessary, to give the next steps, rather than to overwhelm the whole class with another thing to think about.

For those few students, I give a brief overview of direct or cross-examination, depending on which they need. I will go into detail on how to do this in the description of Day 3 below.

Day 3: Questions

On Day 3, the work starts to come together. Students have already read through the evidence multiple times. They have identified key evidence that can support their case or position. They have begun to fill out their scaffolding sheet.

This is the day in which they should work in groups to write their questions. Additionally, this is a good moment to point them toward reading over any stipulated facts (looking for evidence to support their case), general exhibits, and any documents that support the other side's case.

To move them forward on their questioning, I need to provide them with some models depending on whether they are doing direct or cross-examination. There are a couple of ways I do this. The first is to use the same evidence we began to compile the day before when we modeled on the charts.

For the students who are doing direct examination, they need to learn to work backwards. In other words, they have the information they need to support their case (in the left-hand column). Now they must come up with the question to get the witness to provide the answer. I like to give the example: "If I want you to say 'the cat is blue,' then what is the question I need to ask?" We also begin with a simple "name question." How do we get Fritz Herrwerth to say his name? It is funny how often students struggle over that latter one.

Table 2.3 Creating Open-Ended Questions: An Example

Clues	**Information to Help your Case (Quotation or Summary from Text)**	**Open-ended Question(s) to Ask for Witness to Discuss that Information**
Name of witness	Fritz Herrwerth	What is your name?
Witness' job; other key background information	Motorist	What is your job?
Witness' relationship to the defendant	Worked as a driver for Streicher	What was your relationship to Mr. Streicher?
A key date(s)/event(s) in testimony? Witness' location at that date	November 9, 1938 – *Kristallnacht*	Where were you on the night of November 9, 1938?
Reason/evidence #1 from text to support your case	Streicher went to bed early that night	When did Mr. Streicher go to bed that night?

I want students to understand two main points: 1) They need to figure out the question to ask that will get their answer; 2) the questions should be open-ended if possible.

Another way you can model direct examination is by picking a catchy, imaginary case. This year, my ICT co-teacher Myles pretended to be Lebron James and we imagined that he was a witness in a made-up case about whether the best NBA players were using steroids. Here is the beginning of our exchange.

Me: What is your name?
Myles: Lebron James.
Me: What is your job?
Myles: I'm a basketball player.
Me: How long have you been in the NBA?
Myles: About ten years.

In the following student example (Figure 2.2), keep an eye on how Alexander, the witness working with his lawyer partners, matches up his questions to the type of answer that he wants to provide as the witness.

Witness and Direct Examination Preparation Sheet (Option 1)

Direct Examination – These are your witnesses. You need to ask open-ended question (not yes or no) to get them to tell a story to help your defendant. The witness and lawyer doing direct should work on this together using the text.

Student for witness: Alexander

Student for lawyers: ____________

What is the witness' main claim and main supporting reason?

Clues	Information to help your case (Quotation or summary from text)	Open-ended question(s) to ask for witness to discuss that information
Name of witness	~~Philip~~ Philipp Wurzbacher	What is your name?
Witness' job; other key background information	SA leader	What was your occupation?
Witness' relationship to the defendant	Aquaintence / ~~co-worker~~ Head police officer of town that Strecher was governing	What is your relation to Streicher?
A key date(s)/event(s) in testimony? – Witness' location at that date	Nov 9–10 1938: In Bad ~~Ems~~ Em's on account of Chronic laryngitis. Only know what I heard.	
Reason/evidence #1 from text to support your case	"At no meeting did I hear suggestions that violence should be used against the Jewish population"	What type of actions did Streicher suggest against the Jews?
Reason/evidence #2 from text to support your case	"It was repeatedly pointed out that we refrain from attacks or unauthorized acts of violence ... other hostile acts against the jewish people..."	What were your ~~orders to~~ instructions given by your Gruppenfuehrer?
Reason/evidence #3 from text to support your case	Strecher	Who gave that issue to your gruppenfuehrer?
Reason/evidence #4 from text to support your case	The paper was of no importance to them.	~~How did~~ How did the SA respond to the "Der Stuermer"
Reason/evidence #5 from text to support your case	He just wanted to emigrate them without violent acts toward them.	What did Streicher see for the solution of the jewish people

He wanted them to be released — How did Streicher feel ~~about~~ about Dachau ~~feel about~~ and its prisoners

What is your main point that you want to make sure to clarify and repeat?

Streicher is not guilty

To remain on guard and make sure nothing get out of hand.

What were Streichers intentions and strategies during the boycott?

Figure 2.2 Alexander's Direct Examination Scaffolding Sheet

The preparation for students doing cross-examination needs to look a bit different. Here, they also must come up with the question that will get their answer. However, they need to learn to develop close-ended, "yes and no" leading questions. In other words, they basically make a statement and then use a sentence starter or ender to turn it into a question. Here are the sentence stems I use:

- Isn't it true that . . .
- . . ., right?
- . . ., correct?
- . . ., isn't that true?

There are two ways that I model this. First, I might use an example from the actual trial, such as Fritz Herrwerth's testimony. We practice close-ended leading questions together. (See Table 2.4.)

Table 2.4 Creating Close-Ended Questions: An Example

Clues	**Information to Help your Case (Quotation or Summary from Text)**	**Yes/no Question(s) for Witness to Get Him/Her to Admit that Information**
Name of witness	Fritz Herrwerth	You are Fritz Herrwerth, right?
Witness' job; other key background information	Driver	You are a driver, correct?
Witness' relationship to the defendant	Streicher's driver	You were Mr. Streicher's driver, isn't that true?
Lack of credibility (bias) – Misinformation – Lack of information – Vagueness – Inconsistency – Contradicts an exhibit or fact	As his driver, they talked a lot, perhaps were friends	As his driver, you talked a lot in the car, right? You were close? You were close enough that you'd like to see him free, right?
Lack of credibility (bias) – Misinformation – Lack of information – Vagueness – Inconsistency – Contradicts an exhibit or fact	"Herr Streicher went to bed earlier than usual." What time? Why?	Isn't it true that Mr. Streicher went to bed early on the night of *Kristallnacht*? You don't know what time exactly though, right? You don't know why, correct?

Another way that I can model cross-examination is by using an imaginary and easily accessible model, such as a basketball case. What if, let's say, I'm questioning Dwayne Wade about who is the greatest basketball player of all time. Wade wants to support Lebron James's claim to that position. I, however, am the lawyer for Michael Jordan. How do I use cross-examination to weaken Wade's argument? Here's the beginning of our back-and-forth.

Me: Mr. Wade, you played on the same team as Lebron James, right?
Myles: Yes, for three years.
Me: And you were on an NBA championship team together, correct?
Myles: Yes.
Me: So, you were teammates and friends, I imagine that such an experience builds a tremendous bond, right?
Myles: That is right.

I know that lawyers work to get beyond the use of "correct" and "right" in their cross-examinations and instead use intonation to make it clear a statement is actually a question. For my purposes, however, as a social studies teacher trying to teach cross-examination in four days, I actually think it is helpful and important to use those stems to clarify that it is really a statement turning into a question.

There is one other key move in preparing students for cross-examination questions and that is to move them toward identifying contradictions. As I mentioned previously, I try to coordinate the evidence so that that each witness gets two documents that are thematically similar and contain one or more key contradictions. Few things weaken a witness on the stand more than being caught in a contradiction.

I model this in class by juxtaposing short excerpts from two of the complementary witness texts. Let's say that I take this excerpt from Adele Streicher's affidavit.

> From all conversations with Julius Streicher I could see with certainty that he never thought of the solution of the Jewish question in terms of violence, but hoped for the emigration of Jews from Europe and their settlement in territories outside Europe.

I place it right next to an exhibit from one of Julius Streicher's articles called "The Death Blow."

> The twentieth century has the task of saving the European peoples from taking the last step into the abyss. Under the leadership of National Socialism, the awakened German people are leading Europe into total war. It is a total war that will give the death blow to the torturer of the world, Pan-Jewry.

Students immediately see the contradiction. Mrs. Streicher says that her husband never advocated for violence but his writing calls for a "death blow" to Jews. Now students just need to see how to use cross-examination techniques to bring out this contradiction. I use the following format:

- You said . . .
- This means . . .
- But here it says . . .
- This means . . ..

So, the cross-examination model could look like this:

- Mrs. Streicher, you said "I could see with certainty that he never thought of the solution of the Jewish question in terms of violence," right?
- This means that you don't think Streicher wanted to use violence against the Jews, correct?
- Let's look at Streicher's article, exhibit 14. It is from his article "Death Blow." Isn't it true he wrote "the awakened German people are leading Europe into total war. It is a total war that will give the death blow to the torturer of the world, Pan-Jewry?"
- This means he is supporting a death blow to the Jews, right?
- Well, death blows are pretty violent, aren't they?

Susana's cross-examination sheet, which follows, brings out the use of close-ended questions as well as how sometimes it is necessary to use three or four quick and targeted questions on the right-hand column as a ladder to bring out one major point from the quotation on the left.

Cross Examination Preparation Sheet (Option 2)

These are the other side's witnesses. You need to force the witness to make a mistake. **Find a hole in his/her story.** Find another way to see the text. You can lead the witness. **Ask only yes or no questions.** Make a statement that seems like a question. Find ways to **discredit** the witness by exposing bias or lack of information/knowledge. Find the following in the text:

1) Lack of credibility (bias)
2) Misinformation
3) Lack of information
4) Vagueness
5) Inconsistency/Contradiction within itself
6) Statement(s) that contradicts key evidence from an Exhibit or Stipulated Fact

... right? ... correct? ... isn't it true?

What is the witness' main claim and main supporting reason that you want to make sure to address? ______

Clues	Information to help your case / Quotation or summary from text	Yes/no question(s) for witness to get him/her to admit that information
Name of witness T	Friedrich Strobel	Is it correct that your name is Friedrich Strobel? T
Witness' Job; Other key background information A	Co-author of the Original Nazi emigration tax on Jews and a finance offical of the city of Stuttgart	Is it true that you are the → A
Witness' relationship to the defendant T		Isn't it true/correct you was [a] colleague in the Nazi[s], [illegible]
-Lack of credibility (bias) -Misinformation -Lack of information -Vagueness -Inconsistency -Contradicts an Exhibit or Fact A	"I should not have called out this action in this way"	At the meeting on December 3rd Mr. Streicher said, → " ". Isn't it true? ← T He was speaking about the Night of Broken glass, right? ← A
-Lack of credibility (bias) -Misinformation -Lack of information -Vagueness -Inconsistency -Contradicts an Exhibit or Fact T	"he felt that a too quick and radical an extermination of the Jews would put an end also to his own importance"	By saying he was part of this, correct? ← T Streicher wasn't against the extermination of the Jews, he was against that it was too quick, correct? ← A
-Lack of credibility (bias) -Misinformation -Lack of information -Vagueness -Inconsistency -Contradicts an Exhibit or Fact A	"Thereupon I walked into the city and looked around in the streets. People were standing in front of the damaged stores".	You saw Nuremberg after the night of the Broken glass, right? ← T You saw people standing in front of the damaged store, correct? ← A
-Lack of credibility (bias) -Misinformation -Lack of information -Vagueness -Inconsistency -Contradicts an Exhibit or Fact T		You didn't see Streicher put stop to it, correct? ← T Streicher is the governor, he has the power to put stop of it, didn't he? ← A

"It was an order from above, it was an organized affair."

All of this was an order from above right? ← T

218

The person who's above you is Streicher, correct? ← A

Figure 2.3 Susana's Cross-Examination Preparation Sheet

Once I've done these models, students work on their questions the entire period and I run around ragged supporting every student in their first attempts. If I have any professional lawyers who can come to support students, this is a good day for them to be there since it is when deep thinking happens, the time when lawyers and witnesses are really creating their questions, piecing the information and evidence together to make a case, and trying to figure out how to do that in direct or cross examination form.

At some point I call over the one or two lawyers on each side (usually the strongest students) who will do extra work by writing the opening and closing statements. I provide a tips sheet (see following pages) and we go over it briefly. The key here, I think, is that these students do not know the evidence from every witness. So I tell them to go around the room and to talk to the lawyers and witnesses on their side to ask the most important points and evidence that they will provide. This way, the lawyer writing the statements can build a fuller picture of the case and the evidence that they will mount on their side.

Julia's opening statement helps show how a lawyer can presage the main points of their case, begin to attack the reliability of the other side's argument and witnesses, and highlight the larger values of justice that are at stake.

A classroom model is helpful but can only go so far. For almost everyone, legal questioning is a new skill that requires practice and experimentation. Positive results come from giving students time to work (together) and from your constant circulation, check-ins, and subtle prompts to move them forward.

It is often necessary to walk an individual student or small group through one or two examples. For instance, if a student is doing direct examination on Adele Streicher, I may ask him to locate a piece of information that could help Julius Streicher. If he points to the fact that Mr. Streicher essentially lived on a farm doing farmwork during the war, then we need a question for that. The student may try one or two options before ending up with "Where did Mr. Streicher spend his time during the war?"

Day 4 (and/or 5): Final Preparations

During the lesson, three things need to happen. First, it is necessary to go over any logistics for the following day, especially if you are taking a trip: permission slips, where/when you're leaving, etc.

Second, students should work individually on finalizing their questions and doing practice run-throughs with each other, especially if they are witness-lawyer combinations doing direct-examination. Moreover, it is important for

Julia
4/1/15

Honored judges, the man brought before you today is guilty of Conspiracy to Wage Aggressive War and Crimes Against Humanity. The prosecution will prove that Julius Streicher was not only indirectly responsible for the persecution of Jews throughout Germany, he was also a powerful figure during events like Kristallnacht. He organized the boycott of Jewish stores that started a trend of anti-semitism in pre-war Germany, and his actions during the war are a subject of controversy.

Now, the defense will attempt to prove that Streicher's newspaper, Der Sturmer, had very little effect on its countless readers, and those who committed heinous crimes of anti-semitism were not led to do so by Streicher. They would have you, honored judges, believe that Streicher is blameless, despite the many exhibits of evidence that make it clear that Der Sturmer was a useful tool for the Nazis, and changed how the rest of the country saw the Jews. Streicher is in no way innocent of the crimes of others, not when he has brought despicable Nazi propaganda to almost every corner of Germany.

Our witnesses will show that his newspaper was not the only way Streicher brought racial and religious prejudice to all corners of Germany; he helped to organize the boycott of Jewish shops and businesses, which continued long past the designated day and became a long-term trend of anti-semitism. He was the *Gauleiter*, or Party Leader, of the region surrounding Nuremburg when Kristallnacht occurred. Streicher, a man who praised himself for his pursuit of truth and upstanding conviction, did nothing to stop The Night of Broken Glass, one of the most terrible nights for Jews in German history. If the defense tries to convince you, honored judges, that Streicher was helpless to stop this event and was forced to go along with it, I would beg you to remember Streicher's own words, describing himself as someone who stands up for his beliefs.

Lest you think that Streicher's involvement with the Nazis ended with the start of the war, know that the only witness the defense will bring forward to testify to this is his wife, who is hardly trustworthy, as the lawyers of the prosecution will prove to you. We don't know what Julius Streicher did in his years on his farm during the war, as you will see from the cross examinations.

The defense's case will crumble under further examination, along with their unreliable witnesses and weak arguments, as the prosecution is eager to show you. The overwhelming evidence in favor of the prosecution will be presented to you to judge as you see fit. Please think of the faces of the thousands of people, Jews and non-Jews alike, who lost their lives thanks to prejudices like the ones Julius Streicher has encouraged. Thank you.

Figure 2.4 Julia's Opening Statement

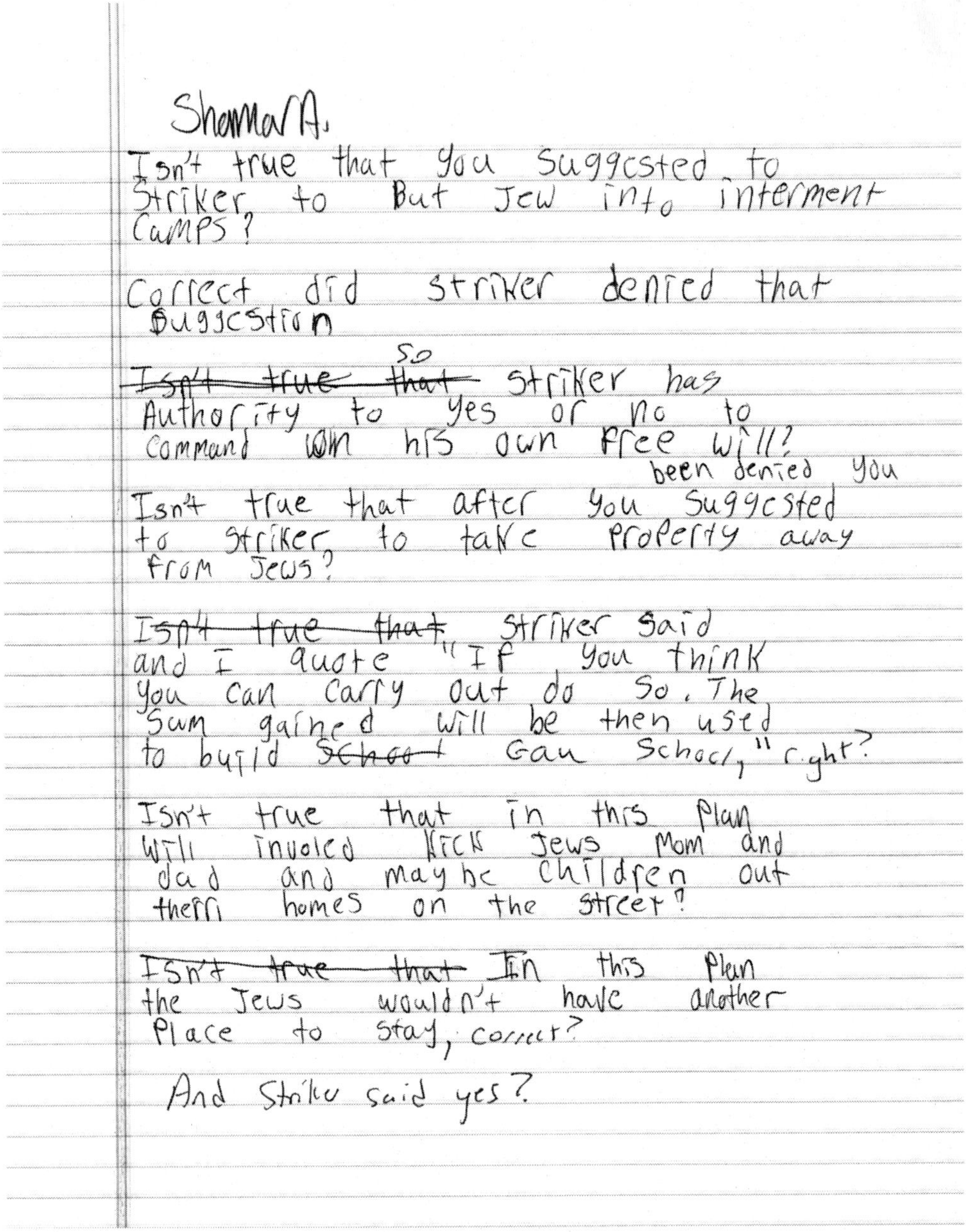

Shamar A.

Isn't true that you suggested to Striker, to But Jew into interment Camps?

Correct did striker denied that suggestion

~~Isn't true that~~ so striker has Authority to yes or no to Command ~~on~~ on his own free will?

been denied you

Isn't true that after you suggested to striker, to take property away from Jews?

~~Isn't true that~~, striker said and I quote "If you think you can carry out do so. The sum gained will be then used to build ~~School~~ Gau School," right?

Isn't true that in this plan will involed kick Jews Mom and dad and maybe children out therri homes on the street?

~~Isn't true that~~ In this plan the Jews wouldn't have another Place to stay, correct?

And Striker said yes?

Figure 2.5 Shamar's Cross-Examination Questions

everyone in a group to have a clean copy of the questions, to ensure that they have the same questions, and to make sure that if more than one lawyer is questioning a witness, they know who is asking which questions.

Third, you need to check in with each of the groups and do run throughs with them on their questions and answers. They should pretend that they are in the trial, sit and stand accordingly, and practice their tone and articulation, as well as the content.

As students actually practice their questions and answers, we notice some gaps in logic, in clarifying evidence, or in actual knowledge of the text. Most often, students will catch issues by practicing out loud that would remain hidden if just on paper. Based on this run-through, students should go back and revise their approach either for homework or during a fifth day of preparation (if you have it).

Figure 2.5 shows Shamar's cross-examination questions, which won the Streicher case for the prosecution. While the sentence formulation is sometimes a bit clumsy, the thinking on his part was top-notch. He set out to first show that Streicher had the authority to stop persecutions from happening, and sometimes did that, but chose not to when a subordinate proposed to expel Jews from their homes.

Day of the Trial

It is nice to have that experience as a teacher where the students (and us) have put so much work into an event that we begin to feel butterflies in anticipation.

There are myriad logistical factors to consider for the day of the trial, many of which are similar to any field trip. You must make sure to check permission slips and get to the venue on time if you are using a courtroom. I always find it necessary to have extra copies of the assignment sheet and witness statements for anyone who might need them plus a notetaking sheet for the jury.

I also make sure to create a brief program of the order of the trial so everyone more or less knows what is coming next. I sometimes bring a videocamera for one student to record the proceedings.

Once in the courtroom, we need to set everyone up in the right places, with the jury in the box and the students in the gallery. I call up the first lawyers who will make opening and closing statements to sit at the lawyer desks.

Normally, I serve as the judge so that I can oversee the procedures and ensure smooth running of the trial. For one class, though, a student really wanted to be the judge (in addition to his other role) so I ran through the process with him, let him take charge, and he did a superb job.

Table 2.5 Order of Trial

1. Judge: Introduction and description of the charges
2. Prosecution Opening Statement
3. Defense Opening Statement
4. Prosecution Witnesses – Prosecution Witness 1: ______________ – Prosecution Witness 2: ______________ – Prosecution Witness 3: ______________ – Prosecution Witness 4: ______________ – Prosecution Witness 5: ______________ – Prosecution Witness 6: ______________
5. Defense Witnesses – Defense Witness 1: ______________ – Defense Witness 2: ______________ – Defense Witness 3: ______________ – Defense Witness 4: ______________ – Defense Witness 5: ______________ – Defense Witness 6: ______________
6. Defense Closing Statement
7. Prosecutor Closing Statement
8. The Judgment
9. Debrief

As I start out the trial, I make sure to provide an opening welcome in which I lay out the importance of the case and the format of the trial. We move into opening statements. When the witness questioning begins, I call lawyers and witnesses up when it is their turn and try to help them through a bit when they're stuck. We finish with the closing statements. At that point, if there is a jury, I ask the members to excuse themselves and try to come to a unanimous decision. If they can't, after 10–15 minutes, they should vote.

Once the jury returns, ask them to share their verdict. There will usually be a cheer from one side of the classroom and a groan from another. One or more of the jury members should explain the verdict.

Lastly, I save about 20 minutes for us to gather around and have a debrief session in which we can focus on the strengths and weakness of the trial and, more importantly, how it fits into our notions of justice. I have included suggested questions for that in my key tips for mock trials.

Table 2.6 Example of Judge's Introduction

Ladies and gentlemen, Today is a day that history will remember. We have experienced the brutalities of the most horrific war that humankind has ever endured. World War II saw not only battles among armies, but also the attempted extermination of targeted groups of people, most prominently the Jews of Europe. We gather today, Americans, Englishmen, Russians, and Germans, in an attempt to move forward by repairing the past. Justice is at stake. Justice, however, is not an easy concept to understand or to fulfill. I invite you today to do your best to secure justice in the case of Mr. Julius Streicher. I ask the defense, regardless of your feelings for him as a person, to provide him with the best possible counsel and defense. Justice depends on that. And I ask the prosecution to speak for the millions of people who cannot be in the courtroom today to make their claims against the defendant. Our Nuremberg Trials have already found some Nazi leaders, such as Hermann Goering, guilty and others to be innocent. Now the hand of justice turns against Mr. Streicher. I would like to briefly outline the charges against him.

How To Do a Successful Mock Trial: Key Tips

1. It is important to choose a witness who is interesting and provides a really ambiguous case of responsibility.
2. Plan ahead to take care of logistical legwork.
3. Make it authentic: use real texts as evidence and real historical characters as witnesses.
4. Get lawyers involved; call up local lawyers to come in on days 3 or 4 of preparation to work on questioning with the students. My students use skype to speak with my father, a lawyer, in Albany. A friend of mine who works nearby comes in for a day.
5. Assign roles based on skill level and personality type. The highest skilled students should do cross-examination. Students with a lot of charisma and the ability to think on their feet should be witnesses. Struggling students work in pairs to do direct examination questions.
6. Meet with students at lunch and after school to prepare with them. Pressure them to come to meet with you.
7. You need four or five days of intense, focused preparation to get ready for the trial.
8. Call a local courtroom ahead of time to see if you can have the trial there. It makes all the difference.
9. Ask friends, colleagues, and former students to join the trial on the day of the event to serve as judges.
10. Do the same trial with two classes so one class can be the defense and the other class can be the prosecution. The extra competition adds a wonderful element.
11. Make sure to debrief the trial afterwards, hopefully on the same day. The debrief allows students to reflect upon larger themes of justice.

    - Was this justice? To what extent was justice reached?
    - Let's compare this to the actual outcome of the trial. Was it similar or different? Why?
    - Would justice have been achieved more if the defendant had been found guilty? Not guilty?
    - Is justice about the outcome or the process?
    - If we wanted to try to achieve justice without a trial, would that be possible? What other options are there? Are they preferable or not?

Table 2.7 Trial Rubric

Learning Goal	**Exceeds Standards (4)**	**Gateway (3)**	**Approaching Standards (2)**	**Beginning (1)**	**No Evidence/ Incorrect (0)**
Claim and Reasons	Establishes and develops precise, knowledgeable claim Provides coherent, sometimes complex supporting reasons	Establishes and develops precise, reasonable claim Provides clear supporting reasons for claim	Establishes reasonable claim Provides mostly clear reasons to support claim	Introduces claim Arguments supporting claim are simplistic or contradictory	No claim is present No reasons given
Significance	Provides a basic answer to the question "So what?" by exploring broader implications of argument	Provides a limited answer to the question "So what?" by exploring broader implications of argument	Alludes to broader implications of argument	Unsuccessfully attempts to discuss broader implications of argument	The broader implications of the argument are neither presented nor explored
Selection of Evidence	Supplies considerable relevant, accurate, verifiable, and mostly convincing evidence for claim(s) and counterclaim	Supplies considerable convincing evidence for claim(s) and counterclaim	Supplies some convincing evidence for claim(s) and counterclaim	Supplies sparse or vague evidence for claim(s) and counterclaim	Supplies reasoning for claims & counterclaim, but no evidence (or) Evidence presented does not seem to support claims and counterclaim
Use of Evidence	Clearly explains how the evidence presented supports, extends, or challenges each claim	Explains how the evidence presented supports, extends, or challenges each reason	There is some explanation of how the evidence presented supports, extends, or challenges each claim	Attempts to explain how the evidence presented supports or challenges each claim	There is no explanation of how the evidence presented supports each claims

Use of Evidence	Clearly explains how the evidence presented supports, extends, or challenges each claim	Explains how the evidence presented supports, extends, or challenges each reason	There is some explanation of how the evidence presented supports, extends, or challenges each claim	Attempts to explain how the evidence presented supports or challenges each claim	There is no explanation of how the evidence presented supports each claims
Sourcing	Provides evaluation of perspective/bias and credibility of sources	Provides some/limited evaluation of perspective/bias and credibility of sources	Identifies sources' backgrounds and credentials	Identifies authorship of sources	Provides irrelevant or inaccurate evaluation of sources
Habit of Voice	Makes strong attempt to take on the character's personality and attributes Speaks fluidly and at proper volume	Makes attempt to take on the character's personality and attributes Mostly speaks fluidly and at proper volume	Makes some attempt to take on the character's personality and attributes Speaks softly and/or mostly reads off of text	Makes weak attempt to take on the character's personality and attributes Speaks at volume that makes it difficult to hear; fully reads off of text	Makes no attempt to take on the character's personality and attributes Does not choose to speak at trial
Accuracy	Correct and specific factual accuracy; shows full comprehension of the case	Correct factual accuracy; shows comprehension of the case	Mostly correct factual accuracy; mostly shows comprehension of the case	Errors in factual accuracy; shows some comprehension of the case	No factual information; shows no comprehension of the case

Notes

1 Herr: A German term similar to "Mr."

2 *Gauleiter*: A *Gauleiter* was the party leader of a regional branch of the Nazi Party or the head of a province. *Gauleiter* was the second highest Nazi Party paramilitary rank.

PART

2

Examples of Historical Mock Trials

CHAPTER 3

Julius Streicher: A Nuremberg Trial

I really enjoyed the Mock trial. It helped me to step into the shoes of Phillip Wurzbacher...I would love to do this again.

(Alexander, high school student)

I liked the trial. I think it was a good way to learn about the different ways that people try to achieve justice, especially after an event like the Holocaust. I definitely know a lot more about Nuremberg and the aftermath of World War II now. It helped me learn about how complicated these situations were, and how it's really hard to find a person to blame.

(Julia, high school student)

Project Outline for Teacher

Background

Julius Streicher was one of the 23 original Nazi defendants tried by the allied victors at the Nuremberg International Military Tribunal from 1945 to 1946. The judges found Streicher, who was referred to as "Jew-Baiter Number One," guilty of Crimes against Humanity and he was executed.

Streicher's main contribution to the genocide was through his propaganda organs, such as the newspaper *Der Stürmer,* which regularly included virulent anti-Semitic writings. He also served as a *Gauleiter* (a regional governor) of the region that included Nuremberg and he led the central planning committee for the boycott on Jewish businesses.

Format of Trial

Following the structure of the real tribunal, the eight witnesses in this project were all actual witnesses in the case or people whose testimony or affidavits played a major role in the trial. Given the length of Streicher's own testimony, I have divided him into two separate witness documents. In other words, one student may play "Streicher 5" and another "Streicher 6." The strongest and most useful witness testimonies are the first six, so only use Strobel and Holz if you have a larger class that requires more roles.

A number of short and pertinent prosecution exhibits are found in the instructions sheet for all lawyers to utilize. All witnesses, additionally, have two documents: an affidavit and a prosecution exhibit. The exhibits generally are excerpts of Streicher's speeches, writings, or illustrations from *Der Stürmer*.

Every defense lawyer is doing direct examination since all witnesses are defense witnesses. Every prosecution lawyer is doing cross-examination. This has an added benefit of making preparation much easier to organize. Moreover, if you have two classes working on this project, and competing against each other, then one class becomes the defense (and learns direct examination) and the other becomes the prosecution (and learns cross).

Key Strategies

The defense should try to use their affidavits to demonstrate that Streicher was a marginal player in the Nazi extermination project. He did not play any significant role after 1940, especially in the planning or implementation of concentration camps or death squads. Hitler had demoted him and "fired" him as governor of Franconia. He spent the majority of the war on a farm with his soon-to-be wife. Moreover, the defense can make the argument that Streicher was by no means the sole propagandist in Nazi Germany and therefore the connection between his anti-Semitic writings and the genocide is weak and/or improvable. Lastly, the defense may argue that in his actual work as *Gauleiter*, Streicher often took the position that violence toward Jews was not the right solution, instead favoring emigration.

The prosecution may attack the majority of the defense witnesses for bias since they all maintained close relationships to Streicher. The lawyers may also use Streicher's own language in many of the exhibits, or illustrations in the newspaper, to invalidate the claim that he was non-violent. Additionally, they can point to *Der Stürmer*'s own words or those of Himmler and other high Nazi officials who laud the newspaper's impact on fomenting German hatred toward Jews. The prosecution needs to show that his work before 1940 was enough to have served as a significant cause of the Holocaust. Much of the prosecution's strategy should be to identify key claims and evidence that the defense will put into play and then to find corresponding evidence in the exhibits that discredits them.

Trial Materials

In the following pages I have included the materials for the entire trial: instruction sheet, scaffolding documents, and evidence sheets for each witness. Rubrics are online.

Principle Sources

The International Military Tribunal for Germany. Avalon Project.
Available at: http://avalon.law.yale.edu/subject_menus/imt.asp

This website is essential for composing evidence sheets (affidavits) for the trial. It has a wide range of primary sources including the indictments and the transcripts of all of the witnesses for the case. All the defense witness statements and the main exhibits come from this website.

German Propaganda Archive. Calvin College.
Available at: http://research.calvin.edu/german-propaganda-archive/

This astoundingly rich website from Calvin College's Randall Bytwerk contains hundreds of speeches, articles, photographs, and posters of Nazi propaganda. It includes a special section of Streicher's work, including speeches as well as articles and cartoons from *Der Stürmer.* This website is indispensable for providing students with primary source propaganda. All the prosecution's exhibits included in the witness documents come from this source, including Streicher's speeches and editorials.

Julius Streicher Biography. United States Holocaust Memorial Museum.
Available at: www.ushmm.org/wlc/en/article.php?ModuleId=10007316

This biography is useful to read with students at the beginning of the trial to provide a life overview of the defendant.

Project Description for Students

Our Question: Was Julius Streicher guilty of "Conspiracy to Wage Aggressive War" and "Crimes against Humanity?"

The indictment (charge)[1] is as follows.

Count One: Conspiracy to Wage Aggressive War

The defendant planned, prepared, initiated, and waged wars of aggression. [He] contemplated, and determined upon and carried out, ruthless wars against countries and populations, in violation of the rules and customs of war, including as typical and systematic means by which the wars were prosecuted, murder, ill-treatment, deportation for slave labor and for other purposes of civilian populations of occupied territories, the plunder of public and private property, the indiscriminate destruction of cities, towns, and villages, and devastation not justified by military necessity.

Count Four: Crimes Against Humanity

Murder, extermination, enslavement, deportation, and other inhumane acts committed against any civilian population, before or during the war; or persecutions on political, racial or religious grounds in execution of or in connection with any crime within the jurisdiction of the tribunal, whether or not in violation of the domestic law of the country where perpetrated. Leaders, organizers, instigators and accomplices participating in the formulation or execution of a common plan or conspiracy to commit any of the foregoing crimes are responsible for all acts performed by any persons in execution of such plan.

What do you need to do?

1. Read sources carefully.
2. Annotate sources to identify evidence that supports your case.
3. Write 5–10 questions for the trial.
4. After the trial, write a 1–2 page reflection about whether the trial helped achieve justice after the genocide.

Who are the lawyers?	
The lawyer roles are as follows:	
Lieutenant Colonel M.C. Griffith-Jones (Junior Counsel for the United Kingdom)	Lawyer for the Prosecution (Cross Examination)
Dr. Hans Marx	Lawyer for the Defense (Direct Examination)

Stipulated Facts: Julius Streicher Case

The following facts are agreed by both parties.

— May 1923 Streicher founded the newspaper, *Der Stürmer*. Over the next two decades, he served as editor, writer, owner, and publisher of the periodical.

— In 1925 Streicher was appointed *Gauleiter* (Party Leader) of the Bavarian region of Franconia (which included his home town of Nuremberg). He held this position until 1940.

— *Der Stürmer*'s circulation was approximately 14,000 in 1927.

— At points between 1932 and 1945 Julius Streicher was:

1. a member of the Nazi Party;
2. a member of the German Parliament;
3. a general in the SA;
4. *Gauleiter* of Franconia;
5. Editor-in-chief of the newspaper *Der Stürmer*.

— *Der Stürmer*'s circulation among the German population was approximately 113,800 in 1934.

— March 1933, the Nazis establish a Ministry of Propaganda and Hitler places Joseph Goebbels at its head. The ministry created a Department of Film, countless posters, and the party's daily newspaper, *Völkischer Beobachter*, whose circulation reached 1.7 million in 1944.

— On April 1, 1933, Nazis staged a boycott of Jewish shops and businesses.

— During the events of *Kristallnacht*, on November 9–10, 1938, Julius Streicher was the *Gauleiter* of Franconia. The city of Nuremberg is within Franconia.

— On August 11, 1938, the Nazis destroyed the main synagogue of Nuremberg.

— November 9/10 was *Kristallnacht*—The Night of Broken Glass. Thousands of Jewish stores and synagogues were destroyed; Jews were killed, beaten, and sent to concentration camps. Nazis arrested 162 Jews in Nuremberg, many of whom were sent to Dachau concentration camp.
— *Der Stürmer*'s circulation among the German population was approximately 473,000 in 1938.
— The box-office hit anti-Semitic film *Jud Süß* was released in 1940, earning 6.5 million Reichsmarks from 20 million viewers. Julius Streicher played no part in this film.
— September 17, 1941 was the beginning of general deportation of German Jews.
— Until 1945, the Nazis killed six million Jews through starvation, firing squads, death marches, and concentration camps.
— The German population in 1939 was about 70 million people.

Prosecution Exhibits[2]

The prosecution has entered the following exhibits as evidence. All lawyers may refer to any of these exhibits as evidence if related to the testimony or affidavit of a particular witness. All these exhibits have been verified for authenticity.

Exhibit 1: M-14
One of Streicher's speeches in April, 1925: "You must realize that the Jew wants our people to perish . . . That is why you must join us and leave those who have brought you nothing but war and inflation and discord. For thousands of years the Jew has been destroying the nations."

Exhibit 2: GB-169
From a Streicher speech on October 4, reported in the *Völkischer Beobachter*, entitled "Safeguard of German Blood and German Honor." He said: "we have therefore to unmask the Jew, and that is what I have been doing for the past 15 years."

Exhibit 3: GB-170
From an article of *Der Stürmer*: "The Sturmer's 15 years of work of enlightenment has already led an army of initiated—millions strong to National Socialism. The continued work of *Der Stürmer* will help to ensure that every German down to the last man will, with heart and hand, join the ranks of those whose

aim it is to crush the head of the serpent Pan-Juda beneath their heels. He who helps to bring this about helps to eliminate the devil, and this devil is the Jew."

Exhibit 4: GB-171

From Streicher's speech in September 1937 at the opening of a bridge in Nuremberg: "It is our duty to tell the children at school and the bigger ones what this memorial means . . . . The Jew no longer shows himself among us openly as he used to. But it would be wrong to say that victory is ours. Full and final victory will have been achieved only when the whole world is rid of Jews."

Exhibit 5: GB-179

From a report of a Christmastime speech of Streicher's to 2,000 children in 1936: "'Do you know who the devil is?' he asked his breathlessly listening audience. 'The Jew, the Jew,' resounded from a thousand children's voices."

Exhibit 6: GB-182

On the occasion of his fiftieth birthday Hitler paid a visit to Nuremberg to congratulate Streicher. From the newspaper *Völkischer Beobachter* on February 13, 1935, reporting on the event:

> Adolf Hitler spoke to his old comrade in arms and the latter's followers in words which went straight to their hearts. By way of introduction he remarked that it was a special pleasure for him to spend, on this day of honor to Julius Streicher, a short while in Nuremberg, the town of battle-steeled National Socialist solidarity, within the circle of the veteran standard-bearers of the National Socialist idea.
>
> Just as they all, during the years of misery, had unshakably believed in the victory of the Movement, so his friend and comrade in arms, Streicher, had stood faithfully at his side at all times. It had been this unshakable belief that had moved mountains.
>
> For Streicher it would surely be an inspiring thought that this fiftieth anniversary meant to him not only the turn of a half century, but also of a thousand years of German history. He had in Streicher a comrade of whom he could say that here in Nuremberg was a man who would never waver for a single second and who would unflinchingly stand behind him in every situation.

Exhibit 7: USA-258

From a letter from Himmler, the head of the SS, published in *Der Stürmer* of April 1937:

> When in future years the history of the reawakening of the German people is written and the next generation is already unable to understand that the German people were once friendly to the Jews, it will be recognized that Julius Streicher and his weekly paper *Der Stürmer* contributed a great deal toward the enlightenment regarding the enemy of mankind.

Exhibit 8: USA-260

From a letter from Baldur von Schirach, the Reich Youth Leader, published in *Der Stürmer* in March 1938: "It is the historical merit of *Der Stürmer* to have enlightened the broad masses of our people in a popular way as to the Jewish world danger."

Exhibit 9

A quotation from a *Der Stürmer* article, edition No. 27, 1937, from Albert Forster, *Gauleiter* of Danzig:

> With pleasure I say that the *Stürmer*, more than any other daily or weekly newspaper, has made clear to the people in simple ways the danger of Jewry. Without Julius Streicher and his *Stürmer*, the importance of a solution to the Jewish question would not be seen to be as critical as it actually is by many citizens. It is therefore to be hoped that those who want to learn the unvarnished truth about the Jewish question will read the *Stürmer*.[3]

Note: On the following pages, you will see how each of these sources is used as witness materials during the trial.

Nuremberg Trial Roles

Table 3.1 Nuremberg Trial Student Roles

Witness Name	Role	Student	Document for Trial
Fritz Herrwerth	Fritz Herrwerth Defense (Direct) Prosecutor (Cross)	________ ________ ________	Witness for the Defense 1
Adele Streicher	Adele Streicher Defense (Direct) Prosecutor (Cross)	________ ________ ________	Witness for the Defense 2
Phillip Wurzbacher	Phillip Wurzbacher Defense (Direct) Prosecutor (Cross)	________ ________ ________	Witness for the Defense 3
Ernst Hiemer	Ernst Hiemer Defense (Direct) Prosecutor (Cross)	________ ________ ________	Witness for the Defense 4
Julius Streicher 5	Julius Streicher 5 Defense (Direct) Prosecutor (Cross)	________ ________ ________	Witness for the Defense 5
Julius Streicher 6	Julius Streicher 6 Defense (Direct) Prosecutor (Cross)	________ ________ ________	Witness for the Defense 6
Friedrich Strobel	Friedrich Strobel Defense (Direct) Prosecutor (Cross)	________ ________ ________	Witness for the Defense 7
Deputy *Gauleiter* Holz	Deputy *Gauleiter* Holz Defense (Direct) Prosecutor (Cross)	________ ________ ________	Witness for the Defense 8
Prosecution Opening Statement			
Defense Opening Statement			
Defense Closing Statement			
Prosecution Closing Statement			

Table 3.2 Nuremberg Trial Source Material

Witness Name	**Sources** Nuremberg Trial Proceedings (NTP) German Propaganda Archive (GPA) Nazi Conspiracy and Aggression (NCA)	
	Witness Materials	**Sources**
Fritz Herrwerth	Herrwerth's testimony. Secret plans against Germany revealed.	NTP Vol. 12.[4] GPA[5]
Adele Streicher	Adele Streicher's testimony. The death blow.	NTP Vol. 12.[6] GPA [7]
Phillip Wurzbacher	Wurzbacher's testimony. "Revenge" cartoon from *Der Stürmer.*	NTP Vol. 12.[8] GPA [9]
Ernst Hiemer	Hiemer's testimony. "The Poisonous Mushroom." "Don't Trust the Fox in the Green Meadow."[11]	NTP Vol. 12.[10] GPA [12]
Julius Streicher 5	Streicher's testimony. "The Way to Action."	NTP Vol. 12.[13] GPA [14]
Julius Streicher 6	Streicher's testimony. "When will the Jewish Danger be over?"	NTP Vol. 12.[15] GPA [16]
Friedrich Strobel	Strobel's testimony. "Loyalty" cartoon from *Der Stürmer.*	NTP Vol. 12.[17] GPA [18]
Deputy Gauleiter Holz	Holz's testimony. "Don't Trust the Fox in the Green Meadow."	NCA Vol. 4[19] GPA [20]

Witness for the Defense 1: Fritz Herrwerth

Directions: Read the affidavit of Fritz Herrwerth, driver of Julius Streicher.

Note any evidence that could be used to show he is innocent of crimes against humanity with Δ. Note any evidence that could show he is guilty with Ψ.

Write 5–10 questions for this witness.

Fritz Herrwerth: Affidavit[21]

I was employed on October 15, 1934, in Nuremberg, not in the personal service of Herr Streicher himself, but in the municipal motor pool. However, I worked for the then *Gauleiter* Streicher.

When Herr Streicher went to bed, I was usually with him or the house superintendent. On that evening, November 9, 1938, Herr Streicher went to bed earlier than usual. I do not know the reason. And that concluded my work for the day. I went from Herr Streicher to the casino of the Gauleitung. That was in the cellar of the Gauleitung building on Schlageterstrasse. I played cards there. And then the former SA Obergruppenfuehrer, Von Obernitz, came and called me, as was customary, by the name of Fritz and told me he had to speak to Herr Streicher very urgently; and I answered him that Herr Streicher had already gone to bed. Then he said, "Then I must rouse him," and he told me he would assume the responsibility; it was an important affair. Herr Von Obernitz went to Herr Streicher's apartment in my car. Herr Streicher's bedroom is above my apartment. I had the keys and of course I could get in at any time.

On the way to the apartment at night I noticed that many SA men were in the streets. I asked Herr Von Obernitz the reason for that. He told me something was going to happen; the Jewish homes were to be destroyed. He did not say anything further to me.

I accompanied Herr Von Obernitz all the way to the bed of Herr Streicher. Herr Von Obernitz then reported to Streicher about what was happening that night. I cannot recall the details very well any more, but I believe he said that the Jewish homes were to be destroyed that night. Herr Streicher was, if I may say so, surprised. He had not known anything about it. He said literally to Herr Von Obernitz, and I remember that very clearly, "That is wrong. One does not solve the Jewish question that way. Do what you have been ordered. I shall have no part in it. If anything should occur so that you need me, then you may come for me." I can also mention that thereupon Herr Von Obernitz said that Hitler had declared that the SA should be allowed to have a fling as retribution for what had occurred in Paris in connection with Herr Vom Rath. Streicher stayed in bed and did not go out during that night.

The synagogue, as far as I know, was burned down by the regular fire department, and upon orders from Herr Von Obernitz.

Prosecution Exhibit 10

This article from *Der Stürmer* was published in 1933 after Hitler took power.

Secret Plans against Germany Revealed[22]

The Prophecies

The non-Jew has no idea of the scope of this struggle. He does not know the Jewish people's secret goals, or the crimes they have committed over four millennia to reach those goals, or the enormous danger it faces if these goals are revealed before they can be realized.

The Jew miscalculated. The spiritual hero did not come too late. He took up battle with Pan-Jewry and won the victory. The world knows the name of this hero. He is Adolf Hitler, the Führer of the German freedom movement. The Jew sank under his blows in the dust. Now the Jew sees the enormous danger he faces. He has been uncovered, his criminal plans have been discovered, and a battle is coming like the world has never seen. World Jewry faces Adolf Hitler. World Jewry faces Germany. The Jews will fight without pity. We must also fight without pity against Pan-Jewry. The Jewish people is the people of the devil. It is a people of criminals and murderers. The Jewish people must be exterminated from the face of the earth.

Witness for the Defense 2: Adele Streicher

Directions: Read the following affidavit of Adele Streicher, wife to Julius Streicher.

Note any evidence that could be used to show he is innocent of crimes against humanity with Δ. Note any evidence that could show he is guilty with Ψ.

Write 5–10 questions for this witness.

Adele Streicher: Affidavit[23]

On June 7, 1940, I became Julius Streicher's secretary and I remained in that job until the end of the war. During that time, Julius Streicher did mainly physical work—that is, agriculture and gardening, and from time to time he wrote articles for *Der Stürmer.*

During the first few years of his stay there Julius Streicher did not leave the farm at all; later, once in a while, he would pay a visit in the neighborhood. His longest absence did not comprise an entire day and never a single night.

When Dr. Goebbels[24] visited the farm, Julius Streicher said to him, "Doctor, you dare to come here? Do you not know that it is prohibited by the Party chiefs to visit me?" Dr. Ley came to the farm on May 7, 1944. The visit of Dr. Goebbels occurred on June 4, 1944.

Both visits were of a rather unofficial character. Dr. Ley wanted mainly to know how Julius Streicher was doing, personally. No political questions were raised. Ley said only, "Streicher, the Führer is waiting for you."

Julius Streicher answered that he had become accustomed to his solitude, that he was happy as a farmer, and that Ley should tell the Führer that he, Streicher, wanted nothing more. At the visit of Dr. Goebbels the subject of the conversation dealt mainly with Julius Streicher's dismissal from his office as *Gauleiter,* and Dr. Goebbels was of the opinion that Julius Streicher should return into the circle of old Party members; but he gave him the same answer, "Tell the Führer I wish for nothing."

They never spoke about the Jewish question.

From all conversations with Julius Streicher I could see with certainty that he never thought of the solution of the Jewish question in terms of violence, but hoped for the emigration of Jews from Europe and their settlement in territories outside Europe.

With the exception of one letter from Herr Himmler there was never any mail from him or other party chiefs. In that letter Herr Himmler complained about the fact that the French prisoners-of-war who were employed on our Pleikershof farm were treated too well.

On the Pleikershof eight French prisoners-of-war, one Polish girl, and one Slovene girl were employed. They were all treated very well and very humanely. Each service for which Julius Streicher asked, each piece of work for which he asked personally, was especially rewarded with tobacco, pastry, fruit, or even money. Such cordial relations developed with some of the Frenchmen during the years that they were there that they assured us, with tears in their eyes at their departure, that they would visit Julius Streicher after the war with their families.

In 1945, Julius Streicher wanted to take part in the fighting in Nuremberg. I wanted to accompany him, so he married me before we left. We wanted to die together.

Prosecution Exhibit 11

This editorial, written by Julius Streicher and published in March, 1943, was in *Der Stürmer.*

The Death Blow[25]

by Julius Streicher

He who lives the life of a criminal wants to avoid being seen as one. His dark behavior forces him to wear the mask of the ordinary man, the mask of the harmless.

The course of world history makes it clear that the Jews succeeded in hiding the great danger of world Jewry from Gentiles. The Jews are masters at deflecting suspicion. They even succeeded in getting Gentiles to believe that the Jews had received a godly mission to save humanity. The Jews owe their toleration to the spiritual conquest of Aryan peoples who converted to Christianity, which enabled them step by step to carry out their plans of enslavement. The Christian command of brotherly love, which demands that its adherents love even their enemies, always caused rising hatred against the Jews to fade into suicidal toleration.

But not always! World history gives witness that the voice of the blood breaks the dam that holds back the will to racial and national self-assertion.

For a thousand years popular uprisings have sought to free people from their torturers. But these popular uprisings lacked unified leadership. In the end, the Jew was always triumphant.

The twentieth century has the task of saving the European peoples from taking the last step into the abyss. Under the leadership of National Socialism, the awakened German people are leading Europe into total war. It is a total war that will give the death blow to the torturer of the world, Pan-Jewry.

Witness for the Defense 3: Philipp Wurzbacher

Directions: Read the following affidavit of Philipp Wurzbacher, an SA Leader[26] in Nuremberg.

Note any evidence that could be used to show he is innocent of crimes against humanity with Δ. Note any evidence that could show he is guilty with Ψ.

Write 5–10 questions for this witness.

Philipp Wurzbacher Affidavit[27]

I was an SA Leader in Nuremberg from 1928. I have known Streicher from meetings, since 1923; personally, from the time of my activity as an SA Leader in the year 1928. At no meeting did I hear suggestions that violence should be used against the Jewish population. Nor did I ever hear Streicher suggest or announce that he had any such intentions in mind.

The SA never undertook anything like acts of violence against Jews in Franconia between 1920 and 1933. On the contrary, the SA had instructions, unequivocal instructions, to refrain from such acts of violence. Severe punishment would have resulted for anyone who did anything like that, or for an SA Leader who gave such orders. Besides, as I have already emphasized, there was never any suggestion or any order to that effect.

I was not in Nuremberg during the events from 9 to 10 November 1938.[28] At that time I was in Bad Ems on account of chronic laryngitis. I can only say what I know from stories, which I heard afterwards.

Opinions were, as far as I could determine upon my return—I believe it was on 23 or 24 November—very much divided. A part of the SA was in favor, the other opposed what had happened, but at all events, the majority in general considered it to be wrong and condemned what had been done.

It goes without saying that after the accession to power, when many doubtful elements joined, the situation was completely different from what it had been before. Up to that time, as a responsible leader, one knew almost every member individually, but now with the tremendous influx of new men, a general survey of the new situation had first to be made. But I believe I may say that an increase of brutality did not occur. Perhaps some undesirable elements which, in the name of the SA, did this or that, had slipped in but in general I cannot say that an overall increase of brutality took place.

Der Stürmer had a very divided reception, I might say, especially among the people in Nuremberg and in particular in the SA. There were large numbers in the SA who, if they did not exactly reject *Der Stürmer,* were in fact not interested because of the tedious repetitions contained in it, and for this reason the paper was of no importance to them. Moreover, it was natural that members of the SA read their own paper, *Der SA Mann,* first.

The objectives which were stated by Streicher were, I should say, unequivocal and clear. He pursued the policy that the strong elements of the Jewish people which occupied positions in the German economy and above all in public life and public offices should be removed and that necessarily, expulsion or emigration should be considered.

I participated in the 1933 boycott. At that time I had instructions from my Gruppenführer to see to it that this boycott should be kept within the limits of order and propriety, and that in this way the success of the boycott would be assured. I instructed the Sturmführer under my command to assign to each department store a guard of two SA men who were to see to it that nothing happened and everything took its course in an orderly and unobjectionable fashion.

The instructions which I received from my Gruppenführer had been issued by *Gauleiter Streicher.*

It was repeatedly pointed out that we were to refrain from attacks or unauthorized acts of violence or other hostile acts against the Jewish people or Jewish individuals, especially in Nuremberg, and that it was strictly prohibited . . .

I can cite one example in which violence was used. I believe it was a small scuffle, at any rate, something had happened, but I do not recall the details of the case. In any event, he called us very sharply to account, and we SA leaders were severely reprimanded and rebuked.

If I may give the essence of it, he said that he would not tolerate that human beings be beaten or molested in any way in his Gau, and for the SA leaders he had rather drastic expressions such as ruffians or similar names—I do not recall them exactly.

Sometimes he could be very harsh and outspoken. At any rate, I can only say that during my activity I did not experience anything or hear anything suggesting that he was a "bloody czar."

He said repeatedly that people who had been taken to Dachau[29] should be freed as soon as possible if there was no criminal or other charge against them. I also know of several cases of release very soon after the arrest of the people or their removal to a concentration camp.

Exhibit 12[30]

The following is a cartoon published in Streicher's magazine *Der Stürmer*: June 1933 (Issue #22).

The title of this cartoon, published five months after Hitler took power, is "Revenge." The Nazi shoving the Jew over the cliff says: "Go where you wanted me to go, you evil spirit."

Figure 3.1 A Cartoon from *Der Stürmer*

Witness for the Defense 4: Ernst Hiemer

Directions: Read the following affidavit of Ernst Hiemer, a German writer, who worked closely with Julius Streicher, the founder of the anti-Semitic newspaper *Der Stürmer.*

Note any evidence that could be used to show he is innocent of crimes against humanity with Δ. Note any evidence that could show he is guilty with Ψ.

Write 5–10 questions for this witness.

Ernst Hiemer: Affadavit[31]

At the end of 1934 I was introduced to the then *Gauleiter*[32] Julius Streicher in the Deutscher Hof in Nuremberg. Streicher gave me the assignment of working for his public health journal, *Die Deutsche Volksgesundheit.* In 1935 I also wrote reports for *Der Stürmer.* Streicher then had me transferred to the editorial staff of *Der Stürmer.*

Eventually, under Streicher's direction and the direction of other staff members of *Der Stürmer,* I did editorial work as a co-editor. The responsible editor of *Der Stürmer* was Karl Holz, Streicher's deputy, but the leading spirit of the paper was Streicher himself. In the year 1938 instructions came from Berlin to the effect that Holz was permitted to contribute to *Der Stürmer,* but in his capacity as state official—he was the Deputy *Gauleiter*—he was no longer to be mentioned in the editions of *Der Stürmer.* Thereupon, on instruction from Streicher, my name was entered in *Der Stürmer* as responsible editor. The overall direction of the paper and all authority connected therewith remained in Streicher's hands, and Streicher retained this position until the collapse.

Streicher wanted by means of *Der Stürmer,* in the simplest and most popular language, to convey to every man and every woman of the German nation knowledge about the Jews. Streicher wanted the entire German people to realize that the Jew was a stranger among them.

Streicher was of the opinion that in Germany the Jewish question should be solved by emigration. He repeatedly criticized the leadership of the Reich because the emigration of Jews was not being carried through in the manner desired by Streicher. When the war came, Streicher asserted that the Jewish problem would no longer have had any significance for a Germany at war if in accordance with his idea it had been solved by complete emigration of the Jews during the preceding time of peace.

Streicher stated his opinion in word as well as in writing, that Palestine and Madagascar would be suitable localities for absorbing the Jews living in Germany. However, he did not follow up this thought, since not Germany but only England and France could dispose of Palestine and Madagascar.

In many circles it was known that the influence of Streicher and of his paper on the movement did decrease. After 1933 Streicher had many conflicts with other party leaders, and he made many enemies. Particularly from the year 1937, Streicher was pushed more and more into the background. Within the party the Institute for the Study of the Jewish Problem, under the leadership of Rosenberg, dealt with the theory of the Jewish problem, and actual authority over the Jews belonged, as is well known, exclusively to Himmler.

When finally in the year 1940 Streicher was relieved of his post as *Gauleiter,* he was completely isolated. From then on he lived on his farm and worked there as a farmer; he wrote articles only for *Der Stürmer.*

This question of the circulation could, of course, be answered best by the publication manager, who was concerned with it. However, I remember approximate figures. *Der Stürmer* was in 1933 a very small paper; but by the year 1935 its circulation increased to about 800,000. After that, however, there was a sharp decline.

Of course, during the war *Der Stürmer* had a smaller circulation. I cannot give you any exact figures and during the last months the circulation of the paper was, of course, extremely small. On the average, I might say that *Der Stürmer* had a circulation of perhaps half a million. Of course, there were special issues which had a much larger circulation.

Streicher himself never told me that he knew about the happenings in the concentration camps. On the contrary, Streicher said he learned of these things only in 1944 through the Swiss press. Streicher received the Swiss newspapers regularly, in particular the *Israelitisches Wochenblatt* of Switzerland, and in 1944 this journal published rather detailed descriptions about what was going on in the concentration camps.

Streicher at first refused to credit these reports in the Swiss press and called them premeditated lies. He declared that these reports were being printed merely for the purpose of undermining the prestige of the German people abroad. It is true Streicher soon changed his opinion. He began to doubt that his opinion was right and finally he believed that the occurrences in concentration camps, as pictured in the Swiss press, did after all correspond to the facts. Streicher said that Himmler was the only man who could have authorized such crimes.

Streicher definitely deprecated what was done in the concentration camps. It did happen that Streicher, in anger—if he had been especially upset by political events—often or at times, asserted that Jews, as an enemy of the German people, should be exterminated. However, Streicher talked in that way only in the first phase of excitement. When he was calmed, he always opposed the extermination of the Jews.

It is a fact that in reports of *Der Stürmer* the extermination of Jewry is spoken about. However, on the other hand. Streicher again and again opposed the murder of the Jews, and I am quite convinced that Streicher and *Der Sturmer* had nothing whatever to do with the happenings in concentration camps. I do not believe it. For it is known now that these crimes in the concentration camps were committed on the instructions of individual leading men—that is, on official orders, and it is my firm conviction that neither Streicher nor *Der Stürmer* had anything to do with them.

Streicher was the founder and the publisher of *Der Stürmer*. But he was, in fact, also the chief editor, and all his colleagues, no matter whether it was his deputy, Holz, or others—all of them had to submit their articles to Streicher before they were printed. Streicher then ordered changes if the need arose; he also gave the editors assignments for articles—that is, he told them with what arguments these articles were to be drawn up; and Streicher knew of all the articles which appeared in *Der Stürmer*. In fact, he was the responsible head, the editor of *Der Stürmer*. All others were his assistants. He himself was, as he often said with pride, one and the same with *Der Stürmer*. "Streicher and *Der Stürmer* are one and the same"—that was his maxim.

Prosecution Exhibit 13

This story comes from *Der Giftpilz*, an anti-Semitic children's book written by Ernst Hiemer and published by Julius Streicher, the publisher of *Der Stürmer*.

The Poisonous Mushroom[33]

A mother and her young boy are gathering mushrooms in the German forest. The boy finds some poisonous ones. The mother explains that there are good mushrooms and poisonous ones, and, as they go home, says:

"Look, Franz, human beings in this world are like the mushrooms in the forest. There are good mushrooms and there are good people. There are poisonous, bad mushrooms and there are bad people. And we have to be on our guard against bad people just as we have to be on guard against poisonous mushrooms. Do you understand that?"

"Yes, mother," Franz replies. "I understand that in dealing with bad people trouble may arise, just as when one eats a poisonous mushroom. One may even die!"

"And do you know, too, who these bad men are, these poisonous mushrooms of mankind?" the mother continued.

Franz slaps his chest in pride: "Of course I know, mother! They are the Jews! Our teacher has often told us about them."

The mother praises her boy for his intelligence, and goes on to explain the different kinds of "poisonous" Jews: the Jewish peddler, the Jewish cattle-dealer, the Kosher butcher, the Jewish doctor, the baptized Jew, and so on.

"However they disguise themselves, or however friendly they try to be, affirming a thousand times their good intentions to us, one must not believe them. Jews they are and Jews they remain. For our Volk they are poison."

"Like the poisonous mushroom!" says Franz.

"Yes, my child! Just as a single poisonous mushroom can kill a whole family, so a solitary Jew can destroy a whole village, a whole city, even an entire *Volk*."

Franz has understood.

"Tell me, mother, do all Gentiles know that the Jew is as dangerous as a poisonous mushroom?"

Mother shakes her head.

"Unfortunately not, my child. There are millions of Gentiles who do not yet know the Jews. So we have to enlighten people and warn them against the Jews. Our young people, too, must be warned. Our boys and girls must learn to know the Jew. They must learn that the Jew is the most dangerous poison mushroom in existence. Just as poisonous mushrooms spring up everywhere, so the Jew is found in every country in the world. Just as poisonous mushrooms often lead to the most dreadful calamity, so the Jew is the cause of misery and distress, illness and death."

The author then concludes this story by pointing the moral:

German youth must learn to recognize the Jewish poison mushroom. They must learn what a danger the Jew is for the German *Volk* and for the whole world. They must learn that the Jewish problem involves the destiny of us all.

"The following tales tell the truth about the Jewish poison mushroom. They show the many shapes the Jew assumes. They show the depravity and baseness of the Jewish race. They show the Jew for what he really is: the devil in human form."

Witness for the Defense 5: Julius Streicher

Directions: Read the following affidavit of Julius Streicher.

Note any evidence that could be used to show he is innocent of crimes against humanity with Δ. Note any evidence that could show he is guilty with Ψ.

Write 5–10 questions for this witness.

Julius Streicher: Affadavit[34]

In 1923 I took part in the first National Socialist revolution or, rather, attempted revolution. It will go down in history as the Hitler Putsch. Adolf Hitler had asked me to come to Munich for it. I went to Munich and took part in the meeting in which Adolf Hitler came to a solemn agreement with representatives of the middle classes to go to northern Germany and put an end to the chaos.

I marched with them up to the Feldherrnhalle. Then I was arrested and, like Adolf Hitler, Rudolf Hess, and others, was taken to Landsberg on the Lech. After a few months I was put up as candidate for the Bavarian Parliament by the Volkischer Block and was elected in the year 1924.

In 1925 after the movement had been permitted again and Adolf Hitler had been released from jail, I was made *Gauleiter* of Franconia. In 1933 I became a deputy to the Reichstag. In 1933 or 1934 the honorary title of SA Gruppenführer was bestowed on me.

I might mention here that I deliberately gave my fighting paper *Der Stürmer,* the subtitle, *A Weekly for the Fight for Truth.* I was quite conscious that I could not be in possession of the entire truth, but I also know that 80 or 90 percent of what I proclaim with conviction was the truth.

A few days before April 1, 1933 I was summoned to the Brown House in Munich. Adolf Hitler explained to me something that I already knew—namely, that a tremendous propaganda campaign against the new Germany was being carried on by the foreign press. Although he himself had only just become Chancellor, although Hindenburg was still at the head of the Reich, although parliament existed, a tremendous campaign of hate against Germany had begun in the foreign press.

The Führer told me that even the Reich flag, the emblem of sovereignty, was being subjected to insults abroad and that we would have to tell world Jewry, "Thus far and no farther." We would have to show them that we would not tolerate it any longer.

Then he told me that a boycott day was to be fixed for April 1 and that I was to organize it. Perhaps it would not be irrelevant to point out the following facts: Adolf Hitler thought that it might be a good thing to use my name in connection with this boycott day; that was not done in the end. So I undertook the organization of the boycott and issued a directive, which I believe is in the hands of the Court. There is no need for me to say much about it. I gave instructions that no attempts should be made on the lives of Jews, that one or more guards should be posted in front of all Jewish premises—that is to say, in front of every Jewish store—and that these guards should be responsible for seeing that no damage was done to property. In short, I organized the proceedings in a way which was perhaps not expected of me, and perhaps not expected by many members of the party. I frankly admit that.

One thing is certain: except for minor incidents the boycott day passed off perfectly. I believe that there is not even one Jew who can contradict this. The boycott day was a disciplined proceeding.

Anti-Semitic publications have existed in Germany for centuries. A book I had, written by Dr. Martin Luther, was, for instance, confiscated. Dr. Martin Luther would very probably sit in my place in the defendants' dock today, if this book had been taken into consideration by the Prosecution. In the book *The Jews and Their Lies,* Dr. Martin Luther writes that the Jews are a serpent's brood and one should burn down their synagogues and destroy them . . .

Even before the coming to power there were in every Gau weekly journals that were anti-Semitic and one daily paper called the *Volkischer Beobachter* in Munich. Apart from that, there were a number of periodicals which were not working directly for the party. There was also anti-Semitic literature. After the seizure of power, the daily press was co-ordinated, and now the party found itself in control of some 3,000 daily papers, numerous weekly journals, and all type of periodicals; and orders were given by the Führer that every newspaper should provide enlightening articles on the Jewish question. The anti-Semitic enlightenment was, therefore, after the seizure of power, carried out on a very large scale in the daily press as well as in the weekly journals, periodicals, and books. Consequently, *Der Stürmer* did not stand alone in its enlightening activity. But I want to state quite openly that I make the claim of having treated the question in the most popular way.

Allow me to add that it is my conviction that the contents of *Der Stürmer* as such were not incitation. During the whole twenty years I never wrote in this connection, "Burn Jewish houses down; beat them to death." Never once did such an incitement appear in *Der Stürmer.*

Now comes the question: is there any proof to be furnished that any deed was done from the time *Der Stürmer* first appeared, a deed of which one can say that it was the result of an incitement? As a deed due to an incitement I might mention a pogrom. That is a spontaneous deed when sections of the people suddenly rise up and kill other people. During the twenty years no pogrom took place in Germany, during the twenty years, as far as I know, no Jew was killed. No murder took place, of which one could have said, "This is the result of an incitement which was caused by anti-Semitic authors or public speakers."

Exhibit 14

The following editorial by Julius Streicher comes from *Der Stürmer*, published in 1943.

The Way to Action[35]

by Julius Streicher

There were certainly minor rulers in the past who came to understand that the Jews are the cause of misfortune, and that only their complete destruction could save the world from being completely poisoned. But this knowledge never led to action. Despite the knowledge that a complete solution was necessary, it was never attempted until the twentieth century, through historic actions by National Socialism.

When at the beginning of the Second World War the Jews again revealed themselves as the arsonists of war, Adolf Hitler announced to the world in the German Reichstag that world war unleashed by world Jewry would end with their destruction. His prophecy was a warning. The Jews mocked the warning, as they mocked all subsequent ones. Now, in the fourth year of the war, World Jewry is beginning to recognize that its fate will be determined by National Socialism.

What the Führer of the German people prophesied at the beginning of the Second World War is becoming bitter reality: World Jewry planned to do good business with the blood of the fighting peoples, but finds itself hurrying toward its annihilation!

As Adolf Hitler stood before the German people twenty years ago to proclaim National Socialism's program, he also made the fateful promise to free the world of its Jewish tormentors. It is wonderful to know that this great man and Führer is keeping this promise! It will be the greatest deed in human history. We are too near the events to praise in solemn worship the deed that has been begun. But the day will come when all of mankind enjoys the peace that it has longed for for millennia.

Witness for the Defense 6: Julius Streicher

Directions: Read the following affidavit of Julius Streicher.

Note any evidence that could be used to show he is innocent of crimes against humanity with Δ. Note any evidence that could show he is guilty with Ψ.

Write 5–10 questions for this witness.

Julius Streicher: Affidavit (Part 2)

During the war I lived alone in the country. For five years I never left my farm. I was watched by the Gestapo. From 1939 on I have been forbidden by the Führer to speak.

I first heard of the mass murders and mass killings at Mondorf when I was in prison. But I am stating here that if I had been told that 2 or 3 million people had been killed, then I would not have believed it. I would not have believed that it was technically possible to kill so many people; and on the basis of the entire attitude and psychology of the Führer, as I knew it, I would not have believed that mass killings, to the extent to which they have taken place, could have taken place. Finished.

We educated no murderers. The contents of the articles which I wrote could not have educated murderers. No murders took place, and that is proof that we did not educate murderers. What happened during the war—well, I certainly did not educate the Führer. The Führer issued the order on his own initiative.

I do not believe that the National Socialists mentioned having read *Der Stürmer* every week. I do not believe that those who received the order from the Führer to carry out killings or to pass on the order to kill, were led to do this by my periodical. Hitler's book, *Mein Kampf*, existed, and the content of that book was the authority, the spiritual authority; nor do I believe that the persons mentioned read that book and carried out the order on the strength of it. Based on my knowledge of what went on in the movement, I am convinced that if the Führer gave an order everyone acted upon it; and I state here quite openly that maybe fate has been kind to me. If the Führer had ordered me to do such things, I would not have been able to kill; but perhaps today I would face some indictment which it has not been possible to lodge against me. Perhaps because fate has taken a hand in this. But the conditions were thus, that the Führer had such a power of hypnotic suggestion that the entire people believed in him; his way was so unusual that, if one knows this fact, one can understand why everyone who received an order acted. And thus I want to reject as untrue and incorrect what was here thought fit to assert against me.

In my province there were approximately fifteen synagogues, in Nuremberg one main synagogue, a somewhat smaller one, and I think several other prayer rooms. The main synagogue stood in the outskirts of the medieval Reichsstadt. Even before 1933, during the so-called period of struggle, when we still had the other government, I stated publicly during a meeting that it was a disgrace that there should be placed in the old city such an oriental monstrosity of a building. After the seizure of power I told the Lord Mayor that he should have the synagogue torn down, and at the same time the planetarium. I might point out that after the world war, in the middle of the park grounds laid out for the recreation of the citizens, a planetarium had been built, an ugly brick building. I gave the order to tear down that building and said that the main synagogue, too, should be razed. If it had been my intention to deprive the Jews of their synagogue as a church, or if I had wanted to give a general signal, then I would have given the order, after the seizure of power, that every synagogue in my Gau should be torn down. Then I would likewise have had all the synagogues in Nuremberg torn down. But it is a fact that in the spring of 1938 only the main synagogue was torn down; the synagogue in the Essenweinstrasse, in the new city, remained untouched. That the order was then given in November of that year to set fire to the synagogues, that is no fault of mine.

Every year the *Gauleiter* and SA[36] and SS[37] leaders met the Führer in Munich on the occasion of the historic day of November 9[38]. We sat down to dinner in the old town mall, and it was customary for the Führer to make a short speech after the dinner. On November 9, 1938, I did not feel very well. I participated in the dinner and then I left; I drove back to Nuremberg and went to bed. Toward midnight I was awakened. My chauffeur told me that the SA leader Von Obernitz wanted to talk to the *Gauleiter*. I received him and he said the following: "*Gauleiter*, you had left already when the Minister of Propaganda, Dr. Goebbels, took the floor and said"—I can now repeat it only approximately— 'Counsellor Vom Rath has been murdered in Paris. That is now the second murder abroad of a prominent National Socialist. This murder is not the murder by the Jew, Gruenspan; this is rather the execution of a deed which has been desired by all Jewry. Something should now be done.'" I do not know now whether Goebbels said the Führer had ordered it; I remember only that Von Obernitz told me that Goebbels had stated that the synagogues were to be set on fire; and I cannot now remember exactly, but I think he told me that the windows of Jewish business houses were to be smashed and that houses were to be demolished.

Then I said to Obernitz, for I was surprised, "Obernitz, I think it is wrong that synagogues be set on fire, and at this moment I think it is wrong that Jewish business houses be demolished; I think these demonstrations are wrong. If people are let loose during the night, deeds can be perpetrated for which one cannot be responsible." I said to Obernitz that I considered the setting on fire of synagogues particularly wrong because abroad and even among the German people the opinion might arise that National Socialism had now started the fight against religion. Obernitz replied, "I have the order." I said, "Obernitz, I will not assume any responsibility here." Obernitz left and the action took place. What I have said under oath here I have previously stated in several interrogations; and my chauffeur will confirm it, for he was witness to this night's conversation, and shortly afterwards when he went to bed told his wife what he had heard up there in my bedroom.

The Prosecution have submitted an article which is a report on a speech which I made on November 10; and that is a remarkable piece of evidence of the fact that the people were against this action. I was forced, because of the atmosphere which prevailed in Nuremberg, to make a public speech and say that one should not have so much sympathy for the Jews. Such was the affair of November 1938.

In February 1940 I was given leave of absence. I lived for five years, until the end of the war, on my estate. At the end of April I went to southern Bavaria, to the Tyrol. I wanted to commit suicide. Then something happened which I do not care to relate. But I can say one thing: I said to friends, "I have proclaimed my views to the world for twenty years. I do not want to end my life by suicide. I will go my way whatever happens as a fanatic in the cause of truth until the very end, a fanatic in the cause of truth."

Defense Exhibit 15

This is a 1942 article from Julius Streicher's newspaper *Der Stürmer.*

When Will the Jewish Danger Be Over?[39]

by Ernst Hiemer

Anti-Semitism is as old as Jewry itself. The Jew was a liar, a swindler, an exploiter, a troublemaker, a poisoner of the blood, and a murderer from the beginning. The Gentile peoples thus responded to this people of criminals throughout history with contempt and rejection.

Over the centuries, repeated attempts were made to eliminate the Jewish danger. Under the assumption that the Jewish question was a religious matter, one attempted to render Jews harmless by forcing them to be baptized. It did not take long for people to realize that this was an entirely false solution. The conversion of Jews to Christianity was only on the surface. Jews became "Christian" only to carry on as Jews.

Jewry is thousands of years old. Thanks to its devilish cleverness, it has often found a way out of nearly hopeless situations. Here, too! The Jews let themselves be expelled without much fuss. They gathered on the other side of the border and waited and waited and waited. They waited for years and decades. They waited for the moment in which the knowledge of the Jewish danger gradually disappeared from people's minds. Then the Jews came back. Then they laid waste to the land more terribly than before.

Today, Europe is ready to solve the Jewish question once and for all. It is thus good to learn from past mistakes and remember what history teaches. And what does history teach us? It teaches:

The Jewish question is not only a German matter! It is also not only a European problem! The Jewish question is a world question! Just as Germany is not safe from the Jews as long as even one Jew remains in Europe, so Europe cannot solve the Jewish question as long as Jews live in the rest of the world.

Jewry is organized world criminality. The Jewish danger will be eliminated only when Jewry thoughout the world has ceased to exist.

Witness for the Defense 7: Friedrich Strobel

Directions: Read the following affidavit of Friedrich Strobel, co-author of the original Nazi emigration tax on Jews and a finance official of the city of Stuttgart.

Note any evidence that could be used to show he is innocent of crimes against humanity with Δ. Note any evidence that could show he is guilty with Ψ.

Write 5–10 questions for this witness.

Friedrich Strobel: Affidavit[40]

On December 3, 1938 at a meeting of the Jurists' association in Nuremberg Streicher said, concerning the demonstrations of November 9, 1938,[41] that I should not have carried out this action in this way. "In such a manner it is impossible to fight a power like World Jewry." Then he added, "What has been done cannot be undone," and some more phrases of that kind.

Streicher frequently spoke against measures and directives of the government when he was of a different opinion, as on this occasion. I had the impression that apparently he had been passed over; for in his speech there was a certain malicious undertone to the effect that the matter was having unfavorable after-effects. I wondered at the time whether Streicher really had a lucid interval and realized how harmful that anti-Jewish action was, or whether merely his vanity was wounded, or whether he felt that a too quick and radical an extermination of the Jews would put an end also to his own importance.

I believe it was on the night of November, 8–9 1938 that that action was carried out. It was on November 7 that Herr Vom Rath[42] was shot, and on the 8th he died, and the night after these things occurred.

I was informed about that action by the personnel in my office. Thereupon I walked into the city and looked around in the streets. People were standing in front of the damaged stores. I had the impression that the vast majority of the population was benumbed and speechless. People shook their heads, looked at each other, muttered something, and then walked away. But, generally, I had the impression that people could not speak aloud, and later I heard that those who had objected to these things were treated rather badly, when they were overheard by informers.

The Russian radio at the time hit the nail on the head by saying, "Let it be said to the credit of the German people that they had no part in the events and that they were sleeping."

The action was definitely not started by the people themselves, because even the majority of the SA men who took part in it did so against their will. It was an order from above; it was an organized affair. The assertion of Dr. Goebbels[43] that the German people had risen spontaneously was an intentional incrimination of the German people.

Defense Exhibit 16[44]

The following cartoon appeared in *Der Stürmer,* November 1935 (Issue #48).

Figure 3.2 A Cartoon from *Der Stürmer*

Title: Loyalty

The sword will not be sheathed.
The Stürmer stands as ever
In battle for the people and the fatherland.
It fights the Jews because it loves the people.

Witness for the Defense 8: Deputy *Gauleiter* Holz

Directions: Read the following affidavit of Deputy *Gauleiter* Holz.[45] Karl Holz was the Nazi Party's Deputy *Gauleiter* of Gau Franconia and an SA Gruppenführer. Quite early on, Holz established a close relationship with Streicher, served under him, and for six years was editor-in-chief of *Der Stürmer.*

Note any evidence that could be used to show he is innocent of crimes against humanity with Δ. Note any evidence that could show he is guilty with Ψ.

Write 5–10 questions for this witness.

Deputy Gauleiter Holz: Affidavit[46]

During the night of the November 9–10 and on November 10, 1938, events took place throughout Germany which I considered to be the signal for a completely different treatment of the Jewish question in Germany. Synagogues and Jewish schools were burnt down and Jewish property was smashed both in shops and in private houses. Besides this, a large number of prominent Jews were taken to concentration camps by the police. Towards midday we discussed these events in the *Gauleiter*'s[47] house.

All of us were of the opinion that we now faced a completely new state of affairs on the Jewish question. By the great action against the Jews carried out in the night and morning of November 10, all precedents and all laws on this subject had been made meaningless. We were of the opinion (particularly I myself) that we should now act on our own initiative in this respect. I proposed to the *Gauleiter* that in view of the great existing lack of housing the best thing would be to put the Jews into a kind of internment camp. Then the houses would become free at once, and the housing shortage would be relieved, at least in part. Besides that, we should have the Jews under control and supervision! I added: "The same thing happened to our prisoners of war and war internees."

The *Gauleiter* said that this suggestion was for the time being unfeasible. Thereupon I made a new proposal. I said to him that I considered it unthinkable that, after the Jews had had their property smashed, they should still be able to own houses and land. I proposed that these houses and this land ought to be taken away from them, and declared myself ready to carry through such an action. I declared that by the Aryanization of Jewish land and houses a large sum could accrue to the Gau of the proceeds. I named some millions of marks. I stated that, in my opinion, this Aryanization could be carried out as legally as the Aryanization of shops. The *Gauleiter*'s answer was something to this effect: "If you think you can carry this out, do so. The sum gained will then be used to build a Gau school." The very same afternoon I began to organize the Aryanization of land.

Exhibit 15: Children's Books

This was one of three anti-Semitic children's books published by Julius Streicher's publishing house, which printed about 100,000. Many schools used the books.

"Don't Trust the Fox in the Green Meadow Nor the Jew on His Oath."[48]

Figure 3.3 A Cartoon from *Der Stürmer*

Here Isaac Blumenfeld we see;
As butcher he makes good money.
But take a closer look, look closely,
A rogue this Yid is mostly.
Isaac sells you meat 'Tis said,
But he gives you filth instead.
See that piece upon the floor,
Another the cat has in its paw.
The Jewish butcher never fails;
Dirty meat weighs more in the scales.
And—please just keep this in your mind
He does not eat it, nor his kind.
Only Jews, to their dire shame,
Could play you such a dirty game!
So listen, you folk, wherever you are:
"Don't trust a fox on the greensward,
And never a Jew on his plighted word!"

Notes

1 Nizkor Project. Web. www.nizkor.org/hweb/imt/tgmwc/tgmwc-01/tgmwc-01-01-01.html
2 http://avalon.law.yale.edu/imt/01–10–46.asp
3 *Der Stürmer,* No. 27 (1937). www.calvin.edu/academic/cas/faculty/streich3.htm
4 http://avalon.law.yale.edu/imt/04–29–46.asp#herrwerth
5 http://research.calvin.edu/german-propaganda-archive/ds6.htm
6 http://avalon.law.yale.edu/imt/04–29–46.asp#fraustreicher
7 http://research.calvin.edu/german-propaganda-archive/ds2.htm
8 http://avalon.law.yale.edu/imt/04–30–46.asp#wurzbacher
9 http://research.calvin.edu/german-propaganda-archive/images/sturmer/ds3.jpg
10 http://avalon.law.yale.edu/imt/04–30–46.asp#hiemer
11 http://research.calvin.edu/german-propaganda-archive/fuchs.htm
12 http://research.calvin.edu/german-propaganda-archive/story2.htm
13 http://avalon.law.yale.edu/imt/04–26–46.asp#streicher
14 http://research.calvin.edu/german-propaganda-archive/ds4.htm
15 http://avalon.law.yale.edu/imt/04–26–46.asp#streicher
16 http://research.calvin.edu/german-propaganda-archive/ds11.htm
17 http://avalon.law.yale.edu/imt/04–30–46.asp#strobel
18 http://research.calvin.edu/german-propaganda-archive/images/sturmer/ds7.jpg
19 http://avalon.law.yale.edu/imt/1757-ps.asp

20 http://research.calvin.edu/german-propaganda-archive/fuchs.htm
21 http://avalon.law.yale.edu/imt/04–29–46.asp#herrwerth
22 http://research.calvin.edu/german-propaganda-archive/ds6.htm
23 http://avalon.law.yale.edu/imt/04–29–46.asp#fraustreicher
24 Joseph Goebbels was a German politician and Reich Minister of Propaganda in Nazi Germany from 1933 to 1945. As one of Adolf Hitler's closest associates and most devout followers, he was known for his zealous orations and deep and virulent anti-Semitism, which led him to support the extermination of the Jews and to be in strong support of the Final Solution.
25 http://research.calvin.edu/german-propaganda-archive/ds2.htm
26 The SA were a Nazi paramilitary police force.
27 http://avalon.law.yale.edu/imt/04–30–46.asp#wurzbacher
28 November 9–10 was the event of *Kristallnacht.*
29 Dachau was a concentration camp for political prisoners.
30 http://research.calvin.edu/german-propaganda-archive/images/sturmer/ds3.jpg
31 http://avalon.law.yale.edu/imt/04–30–46.asp#hiemer
32 *Gauleiter* was Streicher's position. It referred to the Nazi regional governor.
33 http://research.calvin.edu/german-propaganda-archive/story2.htm
34 http://avalon.law.yale.edu/imt/04–26–46.asp#streicher
35 http://research.calvin.edu/german-propaganda-archive/ds4.htm
36 SA: Nazi paramilitary police.
37 SS: Nazi secret police.
38 The night of *Kristallnacht.*
39 http://research.calvin.edu/german-propaganda-archive/ds11.htm
40 http://avalon.law.yale.edu/imt/04–30–46.asp#strobel
41 The night of *Kristallnacht.*
42 He is referring to the assassination of a German ambassador, which was the "spark" for *Kristallnacht.*
43 Dr. Goebbels, Nazi minister of propaganda who organized *Kristallnacht.*
44 http://research.calvin.edu/german-propaganda-archive/images/sturmer/ds7.jpg
45 A *Gauleiter* was the party leader of a regional branch of the Nazi Party or the head of a province or a Reichsgau. *Gauleiter* was the second highest Nazi Party paramilitary rank.
46 http://avalon.law.yale.edu/imt/1757-ps.asp
47 *Gauleiter*: This refers to Streicher since he was the *Gauleiter* of Franconia.
48 http://research.calvin.edu/german-propaganda-archive/fuchs.htm

CHAPTER 4

Galileo and Martin Luther Inquisition Trials

Background for Teacher

This Chapter juxtaposes Galileo's inquisition trial with Martin Luther's hearing at the Diet of Worms. I do them together, one day after the other, but they may also be done separately or individually. Each is a trial based on the crime of heresy. The Church accused Galileo because his writings supposedly propounded Copernicus' heliocentric view of the universe. Charles V, as the pope's representative in the Holy Roman Empire, convened the Diet of Worms to offer Luther a chance to recant his anti-Papal writings.

In order to successfully put on these trials, students must have a prior understanding of the principle conflicts and concepts involved in the case. Words such as "Copernican," "Ptolemaic," "Geocentric," and "Indulgences" come up often in the evidence.

Format of Trial

As inquisition trials, there is only one witness in each case: the defendant. However, to not overburden one student with an insurmountable task, I organized each trial into five defendants— that is, there are five different sets of texts, one for each of the five "Galileos" and for each of the "Martin Luthers."

There are no defense lawyers. Every student is either the defendant or a prosecution lawyer doing cross-examination. There is no direct questioning from a friendly lawyer. There are no other witnesses. In order to build up the inquisition atmosphere, I sit everyone in a circle around the defendant, who is in the middle. Lawyers come up one-by-one to ask accusatory questions. With such an onslaught in front of them, the task of being a defendant is not easy in this trial so I normally choose high-skilled and confident students to take on that role.

Every evidence sheet, for each defendant, includes two exhibits: one written by the defendant and the other by the Church. They are meant to be contradictory documents about a main topic involved in the case, such as salvation, authority, or interpretation.

Key Strategies

The prosecution lawyers, most of the students, must develop cross-examination questions to attack the defendants. Given the charge of heresy, there is a particular strategy for accomplishing this task. Students who are lawyers for the prosecution need to recognize where there are divergences or contradictions between the defendants (Galileo or Luther) and the Church. To differ, in this case, is the definition of the crime of heresy. Since each evidence sheet is composed of one source from the defendant and one from the Church, lawyers need to figure out what the differences are and then create cross-examination questions to illuminate them. Any difference is automatically heresy.

To do this, I have the students first read the Church document and make a list of every main point or claim. Then, they read the defendant's writing and attempt to locate one or two statements that contradict the Church's position. Once accomplished, they just need a structure for developing their questions. I provide them with the following model, which they should adapt. I've included an additional scaffolding sheet for this project that you may want to use because proving heresy is a unique line of questioning.

- The Church said . . . Right?
- But you said . . . Correct?
- These go against each other, isn't that true?
- To go against the Church or the Pope is heresy, right?

Additionally, it is important for the Prosecution to actually show that Galileo and Martin Luther are both experts on these issues. This is an interesting situation because it is not immediately evident that the Church would want to demonstrate that Luther was an expert. Part of the heresy charge, however, becomes strengthened when the prosecutors can show that Luther's crimes were intentional. Since he was an educated monk and a university lecturer he knew what he was doing and he knew his statements and writings were blasphemous from the Church's perspective.

The strategy for the defendants is not easy and requires some creativity and decision-making on their parts. First of all, students playing Galileo must decide whether to stick to their guns and affirm heliocentricity (but argue it is not heresy) or take an ambivalent, waffling position that Galileo was merely showing both sides but did not believe in the Copernican view. In reality, Galileo took that latter course and then completely released any adherence whatsoever to Copernicus. I do not, however, force students to take that road.

A student role-playing Galileo may emphasize the fact that the Church censors approved the book for printing so there is contradiction within the Church. The defendant may emphasize that the Church often uses non-literal interpretations of holy scripture elsewhere in the Bible, so it could also develop symbolic interpretation when it comes to the structure of the universe. Another option is not to take a position on the issue but to point out that heresy would have been impossible since he had never fully accepted Copernicus' view and had followed all Church requirements for publication.

Luther's strategy often needs to be one in which he redefines the definition of heresy. In other words, heresy could be seen as going against the religion or the religious authority. He is clearly doing the latter (as per the Church's view) but according to him he was going against neither the religion nor the authority. For Luther, the religion was about faith in Jesus and he never swayed from that. Moreover, to him the authority was the Bible, not the Church, so his total allegiance to the Bible could not have qualified as heresy. Lastly, his teachings that contradict the Church, such as those involving indulgences, never contradict the Bible. He argues, often, that if anything in the Bible shows him to be a heretic than he would disavow his views.

Law and Order RCI: The Trials of Galileo and Martin Luther

Religious Criminals Investigation

Our Question: Were Galileo and Martin Luther guilty of heresy?

Background

In 1633, the inquisition of the Catholic Church tried Galileo Galilei because of his possibly "heretical" views about the nature of our universe. In 1521, similarly, the Diet of Worms, under Charles V, tried Martin Luther for heresy. We will be transported back to Europe for a combined trial for these two thinkers.

Figure 4.1 Martin Luther at the Diet of Worms[1]

This is not a trial under the American criminal justice system. In this type of trial, there is only one witness: the defendant. Moreover, there is no right to counsel (a lawyer). Instead, the defendants will be alone to answer the questions brought forth to them by the prosecutor. The witnesses have access to the same documents and evidence that are in the hands of the prosecuting lawyers, who are members of the Catholic Church.

For our trial, some students will play Galileo or Martin Luther: the defendants. They also need to write a closing statement for one of them to deliver. Everyone else will be a prosecuting lawyer who has a set of two documents to use as evidence to try to find the defendant guilty. One of the lawyers needs to write an opening statement and one of the lawyers needs to write a closing statement.

What is Heresy?

Heresy is an opinion that goes against established religious beliefs, especially dissension from or denial of Roman Catholic teachings by a member of the Church.

What is the Charge?

Due to what they preached, wrote, and believed, the Catholic Church charges that both Martin Luther and Galileo are heretics.

Galileo Trial Roles

Table 4.1 Galileo Trial Roles

Witness Name	Role	Student	Document for Trial
Galileo Galilei "1"	Galileo 1 Prosecutor (Cross) Prosecutor (Cross)	________ ________ ________	Galileo Evidence 1
Galileo Galilei "2"	Galileo 2 Prosecutor (Cross) Prosecutor (Cross)	________ ________ ________	Galileo Evidence 2
Galileo Galilei "3"	Galileo 3 Prosecutor (Cross) Prosecutor (Cross)	________ ________ ________	Galileo Evidence 3
Galileo Galilei "4"	Galileo 4 Prosecutor (Cross) Prosecutor (Cross)	________ ________ ________	Galileo Evidence 4
Galileo Galilei "5"	Galileo 5 Prosecutor (Cross) Prosecutor (Cross)	________ ________ ________	Galileo Evidence 5
Galileo Galilei "6"	Galileo 6 Prosecutor (Cross) Prosecutor (Cross)	________ ________ ________	Galileo Evidence 6
Prosecution Opening Statement			
Galileo Closing Statement			
Prosecution Closing Statement			

Table 4.2 Galileo Trial Source Material

Witness Name	**Witness Materials**			
	Title	**Author**	**Topic**	**Source Citation**
Galileo Galilei "1"	Psalm 19; Psalm 104; Joshua 10:13 Dialogue Concerning the Two Chief World Systems	Bible Galileo Galilei	Orbits Orbits	Biblegateway.com "Dialogue Concerning the Two Chief World Systems Day 3." *Famous Trials: The Trial of Galileo*. UMKC School of Law. Web.
Galileo Galilei "2"	Consultant's Report on Copernicanism Dialogue Concerning the Two Chief World Systems (Introduction)	Catholic Church Galileo Galilei	Heliocentric model Copernicus and Heliocentric model	"Consultant's Report on Copernicanism." *Famous Trials: The Trial of Galileo*. UMKC School of Law. Web. "Dialogue Concerning the Two Chief World Systems: Introduction." *Famous Trials: The Trial of Galileo*. UMKC School of Law. Web.
Galileo Galilei "3"	Letter from Cardinal Bellarmine to Foscarini Galileo's Letter to Benedetto Castelli	Cardinal Robert Bellarmine Galileo Galilei	Interpretation of Scripture Interpretation of Scripture	"Letter from Cardinal Bellarmine to Foscarini." *Famous Trials: The Trial of Galileo*. UMKC School of Law. Web. "Letter to Castelli." *Famous Trials: The Trial of Galileo*. UMKC School of Law. Web.
Galileo Galilei "4"	Deposition of Tommaso Caccini Galileo's Letter to Benedetto Castelli	Tommaso Caccini Galileo Galilei	Interpretation of Scripture Interpretation of Scripture	Finocchiaro, Maurice, ed. *The Galileo Affair: A Documentary History*. Page 137. Print. "Letter to Castelli." *Famous Trials: The Trial of Galileo*. UMKC School of Law. Web.
Galileo Galilei "5"	Cardinal Bellarmine's Certificate Dialogue Concerning the Two Chief World Systems (Introduction)	Cardinal Robert Bellarmine Galileo Galilei Teaching Copernicus	Copernicus and Heliocentric model	"Statement (Affidavit) of Cardinal Bellarmine to Galileo." *Famous Trials: The Trial of Galileo*. UMKC School of Law. Web. "Dialogue Concerning the Two Chief World Systems: Introduction." *Famous Trials: The Trial of Galileo*. UMKC School of Law. Web.

Martin Luther Trial Roles

Prosecutor: Girolemo Aleander

Table 4.3 Martin Luther Trial Roles

Witness Name	Role	Student	Document for Trial
Luther "1"	Luther 1 Prosecutor (Cross) Prosecutor (Cross)	________ ________ ________	Luther Evidence 1
Luther "2"	Luther 2 Prosecutor (Cross) Prosecutor (Cross)	________ ________ ________	Luther Evidence 2
Luther "3"	Luther 3 Prosecutor (Cross) Prosecutor (Cross)	________ ________ ________	Luther Evidence 3
Luther "4"	Luther 4 Prosecutor (Cross) Prosecutor (Cross)	________ ________ ________	Luther Evidence 4
Luther "5"	Luther 5 Prosecutor (Cross) Prosecutor (Cross)	________ ________ ________	Luther Evidence 5
Luther "6"	Luther 6 Prosecutor (Cross) Prosecutor (Cross)	________ ________ ________	Luther Evidence 6
Prosecution Opening Statement			
Luther Closing Statement			
Prosecution Closing Statement			

Table 4.4 Martin Luther Source Material

Witness Name	Witness Materials			
	Title	**Author**	**Topic**	**Source Citation**
Luther "1"	Sermon on Indulgences 95 Theses #36, 37, 43	Johann Tetzel Martin Luther	Indulgences Indulgences	"Tetzel on Indulgences." Thecaveonline.com. Web. "Martin Luther's 95 Theses." *Martin Luther's 95 Theses*. KDG Wittenberg, 1997. Web. 11 Dec. 2014.
Luther "2"	Unam Sanctum 95 Theses #5, 6. 21–24	Pope Boniface VIII Martin Luther	Papal Authority Papal Authority	Umam Sanctum. Newadvent.org. Web. "Martin Luther's 95 Theses." *Martin Luther's 95 Theses*. KDG Wittenberg, 1997. Web. 11 Dec. 2014.
Luther "3"	Exsurge Domine (Condemning the Errors of Martin Luther) Against the Execrable Bull of the Antichrist	Pope Leo X Martin Luther	Interpretation of Scripture Interpretation of Scripture	"Condemning the Errors of Martin Luther." papalencyclicals.net. Web. "Against the Execrable Bull of the Antichrist." *Famous Trials: The Trial of Martin Luther*. UMKC School of Law. Web.
Luther "4"	"Spiritual Exercises" "Address to the Nobility of the German Nation"	Ignatius Loyola Martin Luther	Church Authority Church Authority	"Rules for Thinking with the Church." Thecaveonline.com. Web. "Address to the Nobility of the German Nation." history.hanover.edu. Web.
Luther "5"	Exsurge Domine (Condemning the Errors of Martin Luther) 95 Theses #41–44	Pope Leo X Martin Luther	Luther's teachings Luther's teachings	"Condemning the Errors of Martin Luther." papalencyclicals.net. Web. "Martin Luther's 95 Theses." *Martin Luther's 95 Theses*. KDG Wittenberg, 1997. Web. 11 Dec. 2014.
Luther "6"	Unam Sanctum Freedom of a Christian	Pope Boniface VIII Martin Luther	Salvation Salvation	Umam Sanctum. Newadvent.org. Web. "Concerning Christian Liberty." Wright.edu. Web.

"Galileo 4" Evidence

Witness: Galileo "1"

Key Idea: Which bodies in the heavens are moving and which are at rest?

Witness:

Prosecuting Lawyer (Cross):

Directions: Read the following texts. Note any evidence that could be used to show that Galileo is innocent of heresy with Δ. Note any evidence that could show that he is guilty of heresy with Ψ.

Lawyers and Witness: Write 5–10 questions for this witness.

Original Title: Psalm 19[2]
Original Source Information: This is a text from the Bible.

In the heavens he (God) has pitched a tent for the sun,
which is like a bridegroom coming forth from his pavilion,
like a champion rejoicing to run his course.
It rises at one end of the heavens
and makes its circuit to the other;
nothing is hidden from its heat.

Original Title: Psalm 104[3]
Original Source Information: This is a text from the Bible.

Praise the LORD, O my soul.
O LORD my God, you are very great . . .
he stretches out the heavens like a tent
and lays the beams of his upper chambers on their waters.
He makes the clouds his chariot
and rides on the wings of the wind.

He makes winds his messengers,
flames of fire his servants.
He set the earth on its foundations;
it can never be moved.

Original Title: Joshua 10 (Verse 13)[4]
Original Source Information: This is a text from the Bible.

So the sun stood still,
and the moon stopped,
till the nation avenged itself on its enemies,
The sun stopped in the middle of the sky and delayed going down about a full day.
There has never been a day like it before or since,

Original Title: Dialogue Concerning the Two Chief World Systems[5]
Author: Galileo Galilei
Original Source Information: This is an excerpt from the book written by Galileo Galilei and published in 1632.

Salv: Now if it is true that the center of the universe is that point around which all the orbs and world bodies (that is, the planets) move, it is quite certain that not the earth, but the sun, is to be found at the center of the universe. Hence, as for this first general conception, the central place is the sun's, and the earth is to be found as far away from the center as it is from the sun.

Salv: The illnesses (mistakes) are in Ptolemy, and the cures for them in Copernicus. Ptolemy's structure is composed of such uneven movements, while in the Copernican system each movement is equable around its own center. With Ptolemy it is necessary to assign to the celestial bodies contrary movements, and make everything move from east to west and at the same time from west to east, whereas with Copernicus all celestial revolutions are in one direction, from west to east. And what are we to say of (Ptolemy's view of) the apparent movement of a planet, so uneven that it not only goes fast at one time and slow at another, but sometimes stops entirely and even goes backward a long way after doing so?

Sagr: I have not, among all the many profundities that I have ever heard, met with anything which is more wonderful to my intellect or has more decisively captured my mind (outside of pure geometrical and arithmetical proofs) than these two conjectures [of the Copernicus' model] one of which is taken from the stoppings and retrograde motions of the five planets, and the other from the peculiarities of movement of the sunspots.

I am rapidly coming to the conclusion that those who remain hostile toward this doctrine must either not have heard it or must not have understood these arguments, which are so numerous and so conclusive.

SALV: I do not give these arguments the status of either conclusiveness or of inconclusiveness, since (as I have said before) my intention has not been to solve anything about this momentous question, but merely to set forth those physical and astronomical reasons which the two sides can give me to set forth. I leave to others the decision, which ultimately should not be ambiguous, since one of the arrangements must be true and the other false. Hence it is not possible within the bounds of human learning that the reasons adopted by the right side should be anything but clearly conclusive, and those opposed to them, vain and ineffective.

SIMP: As to the discourses we have held, and especially this last one concerning the reasons for the ebbing and flowing of the ocean, I am really not entirely convinced; but from such feeble ideas of the matter as I have formed, I admit that your thoughts seem to me more ingenious than many others I have heard.

Witness: Galileo "2"

Key Idea: What is the value of the Copernican theory?

Witness:

Prosecuting Lawyer (Cross):

Directions: Read the following texts. Note any evidence that could be used to show that Galileo is innocent of heresy with Δ. Note any evidence that could show he is guilty of heresy with Ψ.

Lawyers and Witness: Write 5–10 questions for this witness.

Original Title: Consultant's Report on Copernicanism[6]
Author: Catholic leaders and theologians
Original Source Information: This text was published on February 24, 1616. The authors were important Catholic leaders who were called by the Pope to give their opinion on Copernicus's and Galileo's theory.

A decree of February 19, 1616 summoned priests of the Holy Office and required them to give their opinion on the two following propositions[7] in Galileo's work on the sun.

Proposition of Galileo and Copernicus to be assessed:[8]

(1) The sun is the center of the universe and wholly immovable[9] from its place.

Assessment: This proposition was unanimously declared "foolish and absurd; philosophically and formally heretical; it expressly contradicts[10] the teachings of the Holy Scripture in many passages, both in their literal meaning and according to the general interpretation of the Holy Fathers and the doctors of theology."

Original Title: Dialogue Concerning the Two Chief World Systems[11]
Author: Galileo Galilei
Original Source Information: This is an excerpt from the introduction of the book written by Galileo Galilei and published in 1632.

To the Discerning Reader
Several years ago there was published in Rome an edict which imposed a seasonable silence upon the opinion that the earth moves.

I have taken the Copernican side in the discourse, proceeding as with a pure mathematical hypothesis and striving to represent it as superior to supposing the earth motionless – not, indeed absolutely, but as against the arguments of some professed peripatetics.[12]

The celestial phenomena will be examined, strengthening the Copernican hypothesis until it might seem that this must triumph absolutely.

Many years ago I was often to be found in the marvelous city of Venice, in discussions with Signore Giovanni Francesco Sagredo, a man of noble extraction and trenchant wit. From Florence came Signore Filippo Salviati, the least of whose glories were the eminence of his blood and the magnificence of his fortune. His was a sublime intellect which fed no more hungrily upon any pleasure than it did upon fine meditations. I often talked with these two of such matters in the presence of a certain peripatetic philosopher, who I shall call Simplicius, whose greatest obstacle in apprehending the truth seemed to be the reputation he had acquired by his interpretations of Aristotle.

Witness: Galileo "3"

Key Idea: Interpretation of scripture

Witness:

Prosecuting Lawyer (Cross):

Directions: Read the following texts. Note any evidence that could be used to show that Galileo is innocent of heresy with Δ. Note any evidence that could show he is guilty of heresy with Ψ.

Lawyers and Witness: Write 5–10 questions for this witness.

Original Title: Letter from Cardinal Bellarmine to Foscarini[13]
Author: Cardinal Robert Bellarmine
Original Source Information: Robert Bellarmine was one of the leaders of the Catholic Church. He wrote this letter on April 12, 1615 to a priest named Father Foscarini who had taken up and supported some of Galileo's ideas.

To the Very Reverend Father Foscarini,
I have read with interest your letter. I thank you and confess that they are all full of intelligence. You ask for my opinion and so I shall give it to you.

First, I say that you and Mr. Galileo are proceeding prudently by limiting yourselves to speaking suppositionally[14] and not absolutely. For there is no danger in saying that by assuming the earth moves it is sufficient for the mathematician. However, it is different to want to affirm that in reality the sun is at the center of the world and the earth revolves with great speed. This is a very dangerous thing.

Second, I say that the Council prohibits interpreting Scripture against the common consensus of the Holy Fathers. The modern commentaries on the Bible show all agreeing in the literal interpretation that the sun is in heaven and turns around the earth with great speed.

Third, I say that if there were a true demonstration that the sun is at the center of the world and there in the third heaven, and that the sun does not circle the earth but the earth circles the sun, then one would have to proceed with great care in explaining the Scriptures that appear contrary, and say rather that we do not understand them than that what is demonstrated is false. But I will not believe that there is such a demonstration, until it is shown to me.

No scientist has any need to do this, since he clearly experiences that the earth stands still and that the eye is not in error when it judges that the sun moves, as it also is not in error when it judges that the moon and the stars move.

At home, 12 April 1615
As a brother,
Cardinal Bellarmine

Original Title: Galileo's Letter to Benedetto Castelli[15]
Author: Galileo
Original Source Information: Galileo wrote this letter to a friend and colleague, Benedetto Castelli, on December 21, 1613.

It seems to me very prudent to agree that the Holy Scripture can never lie or err, and that its declarations are always true. I should add only that, though Scripture cannot be wrong, some of its interpreters and expositors can sometimes err in various ways. One of these would be very serious, namely to want to limit oneself always to the literal meaning of the words.

In Scripture one finds many propositions which look different from the truth if one goes by the literal meaning, but which are expressed in this manner to accommodate the incapacity of common people. For others who can understand, it is necessary for wise interpreters to produce their true meaning.

Given that in many places the Scripture is not only capable but actually needs interpretations different from the apparent meaning, it seems to me that in disputes about natural phenomena the Bible should be reserved to the last place.

Whatever sensory experience places before our eyes or demonstrations prove to us concerning nature should not be called into question on account of scriptural passages, since not every statement of Scripture is bound to obligations like those of nature.

Witness: Galileo "4"

Key Idea: Interpretation of Scripture

Witness:

Prosecuting Lawyer (Cross):

Directions: Read the following texts. Note any evidence that could be used to show that Galileo is innocent of heresy with Δ. Note any evidence that could show he is guilty of heresy with Ψ.

Lawyers and Witness: Write 5–10 questions for this witness.

Original Title: Deposition of Tommaso Caccini[16]
Author: Tommaso Caccini
Original Source Information: The official legal document outlines the point of view of Tommaso Caccini, an important priest in the Order of Preachers. He gave this deposition on March 20, 1615.

I had been assigned by superiors this year as a reader of Holy Scripture, and I continued with the story of Joshua. I happened to read the passage relating the great miracle which God (briefly) stopped the sun.

I took the opportunity to criticize, with modesty, a certain view once proposed by Nicolaus Copernicus and nowadays held and taught by Mr. Galileo Galilei, mathematician, according to public opinion very widespread in Florence. This is the view that the sun, being for him the center of the world, is immovable. I said that such a view is regarded as discordant with Catholic faith since it contradicts many passages of divine Scripture whose literal sense, as given unanimously by the Holy Fathers, sounds and means the opposite.

I cautioned them that no one was allowed to interpret divine Scripture in a way contrary to the sense on which all the Holy Fathers agree, since this was prohibited by earlier councils.

Thus I declare to this Holy Office that it is a widespread opinion that Galileo holds these two propositions: the earth moves; the sun is motionless. These are propositions which are repugnant to the divine Scripture taught by the Holy Fathers, which teaches that we must believe as true what is contained in Scripture.

By many he is regarded as a good Catholic. By others he is regarded with suspicion in matters of faith.

Original Title: Galileo's Letter to Benedetto Castelli[17]
Author: Galileo
Original Source Information: Galileo wrote this letter to a friend and colleague, Benedetto Castelli, on December 21, 1613.

The task of wise interpreters is to find the true meanings of scriptural passages agreeing with the physical conclusions of which we are certain from experience or demonstrations.

Nature is unchangeable and never deviates[18] from her prescribed laws. It appears to me therefore that no effect of nature, which experience places before our eyes, should be rendered doubtful by passages of Scripture[19] which contain thousands of words admitting of various interpretations, for every sentence of Scripture is not bound by such rigid laws as is every effect of nature . . . .

As therefore the Bible, although dictated by the Holy Spirit, admits in many passages of an interpretation other than the literal one; and as, moreover, we cannot maintain with certainty that *all* interpreters are inspired by God, I think it would be the part of wisdom not to allow any one to apply passages of Scripture in such a way as to force them to support conclusions that contradict our sense concerning nature the contrary of which may afterwards be revealed by the evidence of our senses or by necessary demonstration.

God has endowed us with senses, reason, and understanding and desires to acquaint us in any other way with such knowledge as we are in a position to acquire for ourselves by means of those faculties. God would not want us to bypass the use of our intellect.

Witness: Galileo "5"

Key Idea: Teaching about Copernicus's Model

Witness:

Prosecuting Lawyer (Cross):

Directions: Read the following texts. Note any evidence that could be used to show that Galileo is innocent of heresy with Δ. Note any evidence that could show that he is guilty of heresy with Ψ.

Lawyers and Witness: Write 5–10 questions for this witness.

Original Title: Cardinal Bellarmine's Certificate (May 26, 1616)[20]
Author: Cardinal Bellarmine
Original Source Information: This was a certificate that Cardinal Bellarmine gave Galileo at their meeting in 1616.

We have heard that Mr. Galileo Galilei is being slandered. We say that Galileo has not received any penances. On the contrary, he has only been notified of the declaration made by the Holy Father and published by the Sacred Congregation of the Index, whose content is that the doctrine attributed to Copernicus is contrary to Holy Scripture and therefore cannot be defended or held.

The same mentioned above,
Robert Cardinal Bellarmine

Original Title: Dialogue Concerning the Two Chief World Systems[21]
Author: Galileo Galilei
Original Source Information: This is an excerpt from the introduction of the book written by Galileo Galilei and published in 1632.
Citation:

(My ideas are) deduced from most obvious and therefore most powerfully convincing observations. The most palpable of these, which excludes the earth from the center and places the sun here, is that we find all the planets closer to the earth at one time and farther from it at another. The differences are so great that Venus, for example, is six times as distant from us at its farthest as at its closest, and Mars soars nearly eight times as high in the one state as in the other.

This is reasoned out from finding the three outer planets—Mars, Jupiter, and Saturn—always quite close to the earth when they are in opposition to the sun, and very distant when they are in conjunction with it. This approach and recession is of such moment that Mars when close looks sixty times as large as when it is most distant. Next, it is certain that Venus and Mercury must revolve around the sun, because of their never moving far away from it, and because of their being seen now beyond it and now on this side of it, as Venus's changes of shape conclusively prove. (Note: Venus has phases like the moon.) As to the moon, it is true that this can never separate from the earth in any way, for reasons that will be set forth more specifically as we proceed.

Next as to the earth . . . a motion requiring one year may be attributed to it much more elegantly than a state of rest, leaving the latter for the sun. And such being the case, it necessarily follows that the daily motion, too, belongs to the earth.

Witness: "Luther 1"

Key Idea: Indulgences

Witness:

Prosecuting Lawyer (Cross):

Directions: Read the following text. Note any evidence that could be used to show that Martin Luther is innocent of heresy with Δ. Note any evidence that could show that he is guilty of heresy with Ψ.

Lawyers and Witness: Write 5–10 questions for this witness.

Original Title: 95 Theses[22]
Author: Martin Luther
Original Source Information: This is an excerpt from a text that Martin Luther wrote in 1517 and posted to the door of Wittenberg Cathedral.

36. Any truly repentant Christian has a right to full remission of penalty and guilt, even without indulgence letters.

37. Any true Christian, whether living or dead, participates in all the blessings of Christ and the church; and this is granted him by God, even without indulgence letters.

43. Christians are to be taught that he who gives to the poor or lends to the needy does a better deed than he who buys indulgences.

Original Title: A Sermon[23]
Author: Martin Luther
Original Source Information: This is an excerpt from a sermon (religious speech) that Martin Luther gave in 1517.

The revenues of all Christendom are being sucked into this insatiable [St. Peter's] basilica. The Germans laugh at calling this the common treasure of Christendom. Before long all the churches, palaces, walls, and bridges of Rome will be built out of our money. First of all we should rear living temples, next local churches, and only last of all St. Peter's, which is not necessary for us. We Germans cannot attend St. Peter's. Better that it should never be built than that our local parish churches should be despoiled. The Pope would do better to appoint one good pastor to a church than to confer indulgences upon them all. Why doesn't the Pope build the basilica of St. Peter out of his own money?

Original Title: Sermon on Indulgences[24]
Author: Johann Tetzel
Original Source Information: This is an excerpt from Johann Tetzel's speech about indulgences. Johann Tetzel was one of the main Church preachers in charge of raising money through indulgences.

You may obtain safe conduct from the Vicar[25] of the Lord Jesus Christ by which means you are able to liberate your soul from the hands of the enemy, and convey it by means of contrition and confession, safe and secure from all pains of Purgatory into the happy Kingdom. Consider that for each and every mortal sin it is necessary to undergo seven years of penitence[26] after confession and contrition, either in this life or in Purgatory. How many mortal sins are committed in a day, how many in a week, how many in a month, how many in a year, how many in the whole extent of life! They are nearly numberless, and those that commit them must suffer endless punishment in the burning pains of Purgatory.

But with these confessional letters you will be able at any time in life to obtain full indulgence for all penalties imposed upon you, in all cases except the four reserved to the Apostolic See.

Are you not willing, then, for the fourth part of a florin, to obtain these letters, by virtue of which you may bring, not your money, but your divine and immortal soul safe and sound into the land of Paradise?

Witness: "Luther 2"

Key Idea: Papal Authority

Witness:

Prosecuting Lawyer (Cross):

Directions: Read the following text. Note any evidence that could be used to show Martin Luther is innocent of heresy with Δ. Note any evidence that could show he is guilty of heresy with Ψ.

Lawyers and Witness: Write 5–10 questions for this witness.

Original Title: Unam Sanctam[27]
Author: Pope Boniface VIII
Original Source Information: This is an excerpt from an official document written by Pope Boniface VIII in 1302, about 200 years before Martin Luther. Here he is claiming his rights about King Philip of France, which helped develop the idea of papal primacy.

Urged by faith, we are obliged to believe and to maintain that the Church is one and holy. We believe in her firmly and we confess with simplicity that outside of her there is neither salvation nor the remission of sins.

We venerate[28] this Church as one . . . Therefore, of the one and only Church there is one body and one head, not two heads like a monster; that is, Christ and the Vicar[29] of Christ, Peter and the successor of Peter, since the Lord speaking to Peter Himself said: "Feed my sheep" [Jn 21:17], meaning, my sheep in general, not these, nor those in particular, whence we understand that He entrusted all to him [Peter].

The authority . . . is not human but rather divine, granted to Peter by a divine word and reaffirmed to him (Peter) and his successors by the One Whom Peter confessed, the Lord saying to Peter himself, "Whatsoever you shall bind on earth, shall be bound also in Heaven" etc. [Mt 16:19].

We declare, we proclaim, we define that it is absolutely necessary for salvation that every human creature be subject to the Roman Pontiff.[30]

Original Title: 95 Theses[31]
Author: Martin Luther
Original Source Information: This is an excerpt from a text that Martin Luther wrote in 1517 and posted to the door of the Wittenberg Cathedral.

The pope neither desires nor is able to remit any penalties except those imposed by his own authority or that of the canons.

The pope cannot remit any guilt, except by declaring and showing that it has been remitted by God.

Those indulgence preachers are in error who say that a man is absolved from every penalty and saved by papal indulgences.

Most people are necessarily deceived by that indiscriminate and high-sounding promise of release from penalty.

Those who believe that they can be certain of their salvation because they have indulgence letters will be eternally damned, together with their teachers.

Nevertheless, papal remission and blessing are by no means to be disregarded, for they are, as I have said (Thesis 6), the proclamation of the divine remission.

Witness: "Luther 3"

Key Idea: Interpretation of Scripture

Witness:

Prosecuting Lawyer (Cross):

Directions: Read the following text. Note any evidence that could be used to show Martin Luther is innocent of heresy with Δ. Note any evidence that could show he is guilty of heresy with Ψ.

Lawyers and Witness: Write 5–10 questions for this witness.

Original Title: Exsurge Domine (Condemning the Errors of Martin Luther)[32]
Author: Pope Leo X
Original Source Information: This is an excerpt from an official document written by Pope Leo X in 1520. Everything refers to the actions and beliefs of Martin Luther.

Some, putting aside her true interpretation of Sacred Scripture, are blinded in mind by the father of lies. Wise in their own eyes, according to the ancient practice of heretics, they interpret these same Scriptures otherwise than the Holy Spirit demands, inspired only by their own sense of ambition, and for the sake of popular acclaim . . .

. . . No one of sound mind is ignorant how destructive, pernicious, scandalous, and seductive to pious and simple minds these various errors are, how opposed they are to all charity and reverence for the holy Roman Church who is the mother of all the faithful and teacher of the faith; how destructive they are of the vigor of ecclesiastical discipline, namely obedience. This virtue is the font and origin of all virtues and without it anyone is readily convicted of being unfaithful.

With the advice and consent of these our venerable brothers, with mature deliberation on each and every one of the above theses, and by the authority of almighty God, the blessed Apostles Peter and Paul, and our own authority, we condemn, reprobate, and reject completely each of these theses or errors as either heretical, scandalous, false, offensive to pious ears or seductive of simple minds, and against Catholic truth. By listing them, we decree and declare that all the faithful of both sexes must regard them as condemned, reprobated, and rejected . . . We restrain all in the virtue of holy obedience and under the penalty of an automatic major excommunication . . .

Original Title: Against the Execrable Bull of the Antichrist (Martin Luther's Reply to the Papal Bull of Leo X)[33]
Author: Martin Luther
Original Source Information: This is an excerpt from a response that Martin Luther wrote to the above document in 1520.

Whoever wrote this bull (Exsurge Domine), he is Antichrist. I protest before God, our Lord Jesus, his sacred angels, and the whole world that with my whole heart I dissent from the damnation of this bull, that I curse and execrate[34] it as sacrilege and blasphemy of Christ, God's Son and our Lord.

This bull condemns me from its own word without any proof from Scripture, whereas I back up all my assertions from the Bible. I ask thee, ignorant Antichrist, dost thou think that with thy naked words thou canst prevail against the armor of Scripture?

Whether this bull is by Eck or by the Pope, it is the sum of all impiety, blasphemy, ignorance, impudence, hypocrisy, lying—in a word, it is Satan and his Antichrist.

It is better that I should die a thousand times than that I should retract one syllable of the condemned articles. And as they excommunicated me for the sacrilege of heresy, so I excommunicate them in the name of the sacred truth of God.

Christ will judge whose excommunication will stand. Amen.

Witness: "Luther 4"

Key Idea: Church Authority

Witness:

Prosecuting Lawyer (Cross):

Directions: Read the following text. Note any evidence that could be used to show Martin Luther is innocent of heresy with Δ. Note any evidence that could show he is guilty of heresy with Ψ.

Lawyers and Witness: Write 5–10 questions for this witness.

Original Title: "Spiritual Exercises"[35]
Author: Ignatius Loyola
Original Source Information: This is an excerpt from a text written by Ignatius Loyola, an important priest in the Catholic Church. He was the Superior General of the Jesuits. He was a devoted member of the Church. He wrote and published this text some time between 1522 and 1524.

The following rules should he observed to foster the true attitude of mind we ought to have in the Church militant.

1. We must put aside all judgment of our own, and keep the mind ever ready and prompt to obey in all things the true Spouse of Jesus Christ, our holy Mother, the hierarchical Church.
2. We should praise sacramental confession, the yearly reception of the Most Blessed Sacrament [the Lord's Supper], and praise more highly monthly reception, and still more weekly Communion . . . .
3. We ought to praise the frequent hearing of Mass, the singing of hymns, psalmody, and long prayers whether in the church or outside . . . .
4. We must praise highly religious life, virginity, and continency; and matrimony ought not be praised as much as any of these.
5. We should praise vows of religion, obedience, poverty, chastity, and vows to perform other works of supererogation conducive to perfection . . . .
6. We should show our esteem for the relics of the saints by venerating them and praying to the saints. We should praise visits to the Station Churches, pilgrimages, indulgences, jubilees, the lighting of candles in churches.

9. Finally, we must praise all the commandments of the Church, and be on the alert to find reasons to defend them, and by no means in order to criticize them.
13. If we wish to proceed securely in all things, we must hold fast to the following principle: What seems to me white, I will believe black if the hierarchical Church so defines. For I must be convinced that in Christ our Lord, the bridegroom, and in His spouse the Church, only one Spirit holds sway, which governs and rules for the salvation of souls.

Original Title: Address to the Nobility of the German Nation[36]
Author: Martin Luther
Original Source Information: This is an excerpt from a text written by Martin Luther in 1520.

The Romanists have, with great adroitness, drawn three walls round themselves, with which they have hitherto protected themselves, so that no one could reform them, whereby all Christendom has fallen terribly.

Has not the Pope often erred? Who could help Christianity, in case the Pope errs, if we do not rather believe another who has the Scriptures for him?

Therefore it is a wickedly devised fable—and they cannot quote a single letter to confirm it—that it is for the Pope alone to interpret the Scriptures or to confirm the interpretation of them. They have assumed the authority of their own selves. And though they say that this authority was given to St. Peter when the keys were given to him, it is plain enough that the keys were not given to St. Peter alone, but to the whole community.

I have frequently offered to submit my writings for inquiry and examination, but in vain, though I know, if I am in the right, I must be condemned upon earth and justified by Christ alone in heaven. For all the Scriptures teach us that the affairs of Christians and Christendom must be judged by God alone, they have never yet been justified by men in this world, but the opposition has always been too strong. My greatest care and fear is lest my cause be not condemned by men, by which I should know for certain that it does not please God. Therefore let them go freely to work, pope, bishop, priest, monk, or doctor; they are the true people to persecute the truth, as they have always done.

Witness: "Luther 5"

Key Idea: Luther's Teachings

Witness:

Prosecuting Lawyer (Cross):

Directions: Read the following text. Note any evidence that could be used to show that Martin Luther is innocent of heresy with Δ. Note any evidence that could show he is guilty of heresy with Ψ.

Lawyers and Witness: Write 5–10 questions for this witness.

Original Title: Exsurge Domine (Condemning the Errors of Martin Luther)[37]
Author: Pope Leo X
Original Source Information: This is an excerpt from an official document written by Pope Leo X in 1520. Everything refers to the actions and beliefs of Martin Luther.

Moreover, because the preceding errors and many others are contained in the books or writings of Martin Luther, we likewise condemn, reprobate, and reject completely the books and all the writings and sermons of the said Martin, whether in Latin or any other language, containing the said errors or any one of them; and we wish them to be regarded as utterly condemned, reprobated, and rejected. We forbid each and every one of the faithful of either sex, in virtue of holy obedience and under the above penalties to be incurred automatically, to read, assert, preach, praise, print, publish, or defend them.

All writings which contain some or all of his errors are to be burned. Furthermore, this Martin is to recant perpetually such errors and views. He is to inform us of such recantation through an open document, sealed by two prelates, which we should receive within another sixty days. Or he should personally, with safe conduct, inform us of his recantation by coming to Rome. We would prefer this latter way in order that no doubt remain of his sincere obedience.

Original Title: 95 Theses[38]
Author: Martin Luther
Original Source Information: This is an excerpt from a text that Martin Luther wrote in 1517 and posted to the door of Wittenberg Cathedral.

Papal indulgences must be preached with caution, lest people erroneously think that they are preferable to other good works of love.

Christians are to be taught that he who gives to the poor or lends to the needy does a better deed than he who buys indulgences.

Christians are to be taught that, unless they have more than they need, they must reserve enough for their family needs and by no means squander it on indulgences.

Christians are to be taught that the buying of indulgences is a matter of free choice, not commanded.

Christians are to be taught that the Pope, in granting indulgences, needs and thus desires their devout prayer more than their money.

Witness: "Luther 6"

Key Idea: Salvation

Witness:

Prosecuting Lawyer (Cross):

Directions: Read the following text. Note any evidence that could be used to show that Martin Luther is innocent of heresy with Δ. Note any evidence that could show that he is guilty of heresy with Ψ.

Lawyers and Witness: Write 5–10 questions for this witness.

Original Title: Unam Sanctam[39]
Author: Pope Boniface VIII
Original Source Information: This is an excerpt from an official document written by Pope Boniface VIII in 1302, about 200 years before Martin Luther. Here he is claiming his rights over King Philip of France, which helped develop the idea of papal primacy.

Urged by faith, we are obliged to believe and to maintain that the Church is one and holy. We believe in her firmly and we confess with simplicity that outside of her there is neither salvation nor the remission of sins.

We declare, we proclaim, we define that it is absolutely necessary for salvation that every human creature be subject to the Roman Pontiff.[40]

Original Title: The Freedom of a Christian[41]
Author: Martin Luther
Original Source Information: This is an excerpt from an official document written by Martin Luther.

And, to cast everything aside, even speculations, meditations, and whatever things can be performed by the exertions of the soul itself, are of no profit. One thing, and one alone, is necessary for life, justification, and Christian liberty; and that is the most holy word of God, the Gospel of Christ . . . For faith alone, and the efficacious use of the word of God, bring salvation . . . .

Since then this faith can reign only in the inward man . . . and since it alone justifies, it is evident that by no outward work or labor can the inward man be at all justified, made free, and saved; and that no works whatever have any relation to him. And so, on the other hand, it is solely by impiety and incredulity of heart that he becomes guilty and a slave of sin, deserving condemnation, not by any outward sin or work . . .

Notes

1. http://en.wikipedia.org/wiki/Diet_of_Worms
2. www.biblegateway.com
3. www.biblegateway.com
4. www.biblegateway.com
5. "Dialogue Concerning the Two Chief World Systems Day 3." *Famous Trials: The Trial of Galileo.* UMKC School of Law. Web.
6. "Consultant's Report on Copernicanism." *Famous Trials: The Trial of Galileo.* UMKC School of Law. Web.
7. Arguments.
8. Evaluated.
8. Cannot be moved.
10. Goes against.
11. "Dialogue Concerning the Two Chief World Systems: Introduction." *Famous Trials: The Trial of Galileo.* UMKC School of Law. Web.
12. Peripatetics = philosophers who followed the views of the ancient Greeks (i.e. Ptolemy's view).
13. "Letter from Cardinal Bellarmine to Foscarini." *Famous Trials: The Trial of Galileo.* UMKC School of Law. Web.
14. Suppositionally = tentatively; not with total certainty; hypothetically.
15. "Letter to Castelli." *Famous Trials: The Trial of Galileo.* UMKC School of Law. Web.
16. Finocchiaro, Maurice, ed. *The Galileo Affair: A Documentary History*, p. 137. Print.
17. "Letter to Castelli." *Famous Trials: The Trial of Galileo.* UMKC School of Law. Web.
18. Goes away from.
19. Bible.
20. "Statement (Affidavit) of Cardinal Bellarmine to Galileo." *Famous Trials: The Trial of Galileo.* UMKC School of Law. Web.
21. "Dialogue Concerning the Two Chief World Systems: Introduction." *Famous Trials: The Trial of Galileo.* UMKC School of Law. Web.
22. "Martin Luther's 95 Theses." *Martin Luther's 95 Theses.* KDG Wittenberg, 1997. Web. December 11, 2014.
23. Bainton, Roland H. *Here I Stand: A Life of Martin Luther.* Reprint. London: Forgotten Books, 2013. 80–1. Print.
24. "Tetzel on Indulgences." Thecaveonline.com. Web.

25. A representative (the "vicar" of Jesus is the Pope).
26. Penitence = the action of showing you are sorry.
27. Unam Sanctam. Newadvent.org. Web.
28. Venerate = honor.
29. Vicar = representative.
30. Pontiff = Pope.
31. "Martin Luther's 95 Theses." *Martin Luther's 95 Theses.* KDG Wittenberg, 1997. Web. December 11, 2014.
32. "Condemning the Errors of Martin Luther." papalencyclicals.net. Web.
33. "Against the Execrable Bull of the Antichrist." *Famous Trials: The Trial of Martin Luther.* UMKC School of Law. Web.
34. Execrate = to loath, to hate.
35. "Rules for Thinking with the Church." Thecaveonline.com. Web.
36. "Address to the Nobility of the German Nation." history.hanover.edu. Web.
37. "Condemning the Errors of Martin Luther." papalencyclicals.net. Web.
38. "Martin Luther's 95 Theses." *Martin Luther's 95 Theses.* KDG Wittenberg, 1997. Web. December 11, 2014.
39. Unam Sanctam. Newadvent.org. Web.
40. Pontiff = Pope.
41. "Concerning Christian Liberty." Wright.edu. Web.

PART

3

Examples of Literary Mock Trials

CHAPTER 5 *To Kill a Mockingbird* Trial

> The mock trial showed me what a witness went through. All the questions and responsibility that a witness has to face can be really stressful and that's not something you can learn from a book.
>
> (Carlos, high school student)

To Kill a Mockingbird, the canonical novel by Harper Lee, presents a somewhat unique opportunity to engage in a mock trial in an English Literature or Humanities class. It sometimes seems almost as if the only unifying experience in the American educational system is the use of *To Kill a Mockingbird* in a middle- or high-school classroom. We all are touched in some way by the story of Scout's childhood and the ways in which an event like Tom Robinson's trial can shape a community.

Given its ubiquitous presence in the American classroom, there are countless wonderful ways to teach the novel. Here, I present a mock trial format as one successful method to engage students into the second half of the text, when the trial takes place in the Maycomb county courthouse. I will not delve into the core strategies for mock trials that I outline in Chapters 1–2, but rather some specifics about bringing this case to life.

A mock trial of *To Kill a Mockingbird* does present some unique challenges, most significantly in the language that is used in the courtroom, in the nature of the crime (rape), and in the paucity of witnesses. Regarding the first two issues, it is certain that each teacher must make a choice about whether the students in that classroom have the emotional maturity to handle the situation. My recommendation is that a discussion must take place prior to beginning the trial about the type of language that will be acceptable for this simulation, given the ways in which some of the white characters refer to African-Americans in the novel. Equally important, it may be necessary to consider which student(s) you might cast as Mayella Ewell and have a discussion with him or her about whether they feel comfortable talking about issues of sexual violence and rape. We can never be sure about the ways in which these topics can serve as emotional triggers because of prior experiences.

If you decide that this trial is doable, then I think implementing it will add a rich layer to the study of the book, especially in a classroom where students are trying to understand the text both as a work of literature and as an historical lens to understand the racial injustices and bigotry of twentieth-century America. Like any role-play, it will transform student understanding of the characters, their motivations, and their feelings.

The third challenge that I mentioned involves the lack of characters. Unlike other trials in this book, here we are working off of only four witnesses: Heck Tate, Bob Ewell, Mayella Ewell, and Tom Robinson. If you add in the two lawyers, Atticus Finch and Mr. Gilmer, then you have only six roles to work with.

There are a few ways to make this work. One option, of course, is to have a group of students work together on each role and to choose one or two of them to present at the trial. Another possibility is to make the trial one of a few menu options for a class project. In other words, some students choose to take part in the trial while others work on a different assignment, like an essay, journalism report, literary analysis, painting, or the like. In this case, those students who work on another option could become jury members in the trial.

The creation of source sheets, or affidavits, for witnesses for this trial was an interesting exercise that could be used for any other piece of literature that includes a trial, such as the *The Stranger, Lincoln Lawyer* or *A Time to Kill.* In this case, the script was there, in the book. Similar to what I described for the Nuremberg trial, the task was to piece the statements together in a way that would leave thinking to be done by the students, whether as lawyers or witnesses. To do this, you can type up the witnesses' statements directly from the book, leaving out the questions asked by Atticus Finch or Mr. Gilmer or any of the intervening narration or dialogue spoken by some of the observers, such as Scout. As I did this, I paid close attention to the questions being asked by the lawyers in order to make sure the answers made sense. For example, in the situations in which the lawyer asked a "yes" or "no" question, and the response was simply "yes," then I stuck as closely as possible to the wording of the question in order to form the answer. It is also possible to find scripts of the full trial online, which you can then edit.

There were a few other key moves that were necessary. First, Atticus Finch's language is, of course, quite distinct from Tom Robinson's. If I had to use one of Atticus's questions to flesh out Tom Robinson's statement, then I had to make the judgment about what type of vocabulary to use. Whenever possible, I went for something neutral that maintained the integrity of the idea, skewing

Table 5.1 Creating the Witness Statement: An Example

Actual Text	Witness Statement
Atticus: Didn't call a doctor? Tate: No, sir. Atticus: Why not? Tate: Well, I can tell you why I didn't. It wasn't necessary, Mr. Finch. She was mighty banged up. Something sho' happened; it was obvious.	Tate: I can tell you why I didn't call a doctor. It wasn't necessary. She was mighty banged up. Something sho' happened; it was obvious.

neither for Atticus' lofty rhetoric or my imagination of what Tom Robinson's phrasing might be.

There were also many points where, in order to make it seem like an affidavit rather than a statement in the courtroom answering a lawyer's question, I took out phrasings like "sir" or "suh" or "Yes, Mr. Finch." Here's an example of the actual text from the book and then how it comes out in our witness statement.

With the witness statements extracted and adapted from the book, the classroom mock trial is ready to go just as any of the historical mock trials that I described in previous chapters. One of the interesting opportunities available with a literature trial is then to compare the questions that the students compose with those of the lawyers in the book. This can be combined with a comparison of how we would imagine a character like Scout responds to our classroom trial with her responses to the one in the pages of Harper Lee's masterpiece.

It is certainly more common to find a mock trial in a social studies curriculum than an English one. My hope is by providing this *To Kill a Mockingbird* case English teachers will also see the potential for increasing student engagement and learning in their own classrooms. And, it is important to mention, *To Kill a Mockingbird* is by no means the only option. Many literature teachers who put together a contemporary fiction course might opt for something like "Crime and Justice" as a lens, especially with the proliferation of courtroom novels in the past decade. Whether they choose something like John Grisham's *A Time to Kill* or Michael Connelly's *The Lincoln Lawyer*, the same process that went into composing the witness statements for *To Kill a Mockingbird* can be adapted for those books.

To Kill a Mockingbird Trial Roles: The Prosecution's Case

Table 5.2 To Kill a Mockingbird Trial Roles: The Prosecution's Case

Witness Name	Role	Student	Document for Trial
Heck Tate	Heck Tate Prosecutor (Direct) Defense (Cross)	__________ __________ __________	Witness for the Prosecution 1
Bob Ewell	Bob Ewell Prosecutor (Direct) Defense (Cross)	__________ __________ __________	Witness for the Prosecution 2
Mayella Ewell	Mayella Ewell Prosecutor (Direct) Defense (Cross)	__________ __________ __________	Witness for the Prosecution 3
Prosecution Opening Statement			
Prosecution Closing Statement			

To Kill a Mockingbird Trial Roles: The Defense's Case

Table 5.3 To Kill a Mockingbird Trial Roles: The Defense's Case

Witness Name	Role	Student	Document for Trial
Tom Robinson	Tom Robinson Defense (Direct) Prosecutor (Cross)	__________ __________ __________	Witness for the Defense 1
Defense Opening Statement			
Defense Closing Statement			

Witness for the Prosecution 1: Heck Tate

Key Idea: Heck Tate is the county sheriff who was called by the family after Mayella was found injured.

Witness:

Prosecuting Lawyer (Direct):

Defense Lawyer (Cross):

Directions: Read the following affidavit of Heck Tate, county sheriff. Note any evidence that could be used to show that Tom Robinson is guilty of rape with Ψ. Note any evidence that he is not guilty of rape with Δ.

Source: *To Kill a Mockingbird*

I was fetched by bob—by Mr. Bob Ewell yonder, one night—It was the night of November twenty-first. I was just leaving my office to go home when B—Mr. Ewell come in, very excited he was, and said get out to his house quick, some n_'d raped his girl. Got in the car and went out as fast as I could.

Found her lying on the floor in the middle of the front room, one on the right as you go in. She was pretty well beat up, but I helped her to her feet and she washed her face in a bucket in the corner and said she was all right. I asked her who hurt her, and she said it was Tom Robinson—Asked her if he took advantage of her, and she said, "Yes, he did." So I went down to Robinson's house and brought him back. She identified him as the one, so I took him in. That's all there was to it. I can tell you why I didn't (call a doctor). It wasn't necessary. She was mighty banged up. Something sho' happened; it was obvious.

Well, she was beaten around the head. There was already bruises comin' on her arms, and it happened about thirty minutes before—that's what they said. Anyway, she was pretty bruised up when I got there, and she had a black eye comin'.

Let's see . . . Her left; (No), that'd make it her right. It was her right eye. I remember now. She was bunged up on that side of her face . . . It was her right eye, I said. I remember now. She was bunged up on that side of her face. The right side, Mr. Finch, but she had more bruises—Her arms were bruised, and she showed me her neck. There were definite finger marks on her gullet—I'd say they were all around. She had a small throat; anybody could'a reached around it with—

CHAPTER 6

Imaginary Literary Trials

I think mock trials are a good way to learn because they're very interactive . . . . The mock trials helped me to understand how to achieve justice.

(Nolan, high school student)

Background

When working on historical trials, I emphasize historical accuracy. Whereas some teachers engage their students in hypothetical cases, I prefer to use ones that actually took place. The realm of literature and fiction, on the other hand, presents a broader spectrum of opportunities for trials. If the author is creating a fictional world, why should we not create a fictional trial?

This chapter presents a wider array of choices for mock trials than the type offered by the *To Kill a Mockingbird* model. In the latter example, we depend on the author to create an actual trial within the text and we then take advantage of it to develop and execute our own trial (before we find out the result in the book). The imaginary trial, meanwhile, becomes an extension of the text, the type of creative project in the vein of asking students to write a new ending to the story or the next chapter of the book.

We know that "evaluation" is high on Bloom's Taxonomy. An imaginary trial is really about evaluating a character and her motivations and actions by analyzing language in the text. We are trying to look deeply into that character's actions and words to understand her better, to evaluate her innocence or guilt in relation to a particular crime, and to use our reading of the text to make a judgment.

The key strategy to make this happen is to identify a piece of literature in which a central character finds himself or herself in a morally ambiguous choice, which allows us to delve deeply into the meaning and consequences of the resulting decisions. It may be a case in which a character steals to feed his family, like Jean Valjean in *Les Misérables*. Or it may be an instance in which someone kills a friend or family member to actually help him, such as George's killing of Lenny in *Of Mice and Men*. Conceivably, the "crime" could be one that is not even a true crime in the books. Perhaps George is on trial not for killing Lenny but rather for being a bad friend or perhaps Jean Valjean is on trial for lying.

Once we have the book, the possible "crime," and the identity of the defendant, our next step is to determine the pages in the book that relate to that particular crime and the likely witnesses who could speak to those actions. I try to go back to the book and highlight key passages that relate to the crime and identify characters in the book to be the witnesses for those sections. By doing so, we not only think through the proceedings of the trial ahead of time and select the most meaningful evidence, but we also provide excellent scaffolding to students by providing one step of the puzzle: which part of the book to re-read.

At this point, much of my logistical thinking around a particular project becomes similar to how I would approach an historical mock trial. I place the highest performing students in the roles that require the most work or the most demanding work, whether as the defendant (who must master all of the text) or as a lawyer doing cross-examination.

In the following section, I will use a trial based around Steinbeck's novel *The Pearl* to clarify how these steps play out in practice. I also include the assignment and scaffolding sheets.

The Pearl Trial[1]

The classroom trial for *The Pearl* should take place after the students have finished reading the book and are ready to fully evaluate Kino's actions, his motivations, and his level of responsibility for Coyotito's death. To summarize the plot: Kino, a poor indigenous pearl diver in Mexico, has recently found the "pearl of the world," perhaps the most valuable jewel ever encountered in his town. He and his wife Juana dream of using it to finance a real education for their son, Coyotito, in order to elevate him out of their social class. The pearl, however, cultivates jealousy within the community and begins to be a magnet for danger. When unknown coveters attack Kino, Juana begins to beg him to get rid of the pearl. Dreaming big, he holds on to it, against her protests, even as the danger increases and divisions erupt within their marriage. After Kino kills an attacker, the three go on the run but are followed by trackers. In the end, Kino attempts to protect his family but the trackers shoot and kill Coyotito, leading Kino to finally throw the pearl back into the ocean.

The trial evaluates Kino's choices and whether or not he should be held responsible for Coyotito's death. In this sense, it results in close-reading to delve further into Kino's motivations and choices as well as the way that Steinbeck uses language to shape the internal conflict, Kino's growing obsession with the pearl, and the contrasting views of the best way to ensure the well-being of their family.

Format of the Trial

While the book takes place in Mexico, I find it more helpful to frame the trial around the American criminal justice system. Doing so makes it more familiar and more useful to the students, and I'm not sure that dealing with the technical differences between American and Mexican legal processes holds considerable value for the learning.

This trial, like *To Kill a Mockingbird,* includes both defense and prosecution witnesses. Consequently, it is important to carefully choose which students will take on which roles. Any task that includes creating cross-examination questions will likely be more difficult. A high-achieving student should also take on the role of Kino.

Key Strategies

Students will need to close-read their sections of the text to grapple with the language that Steinbeck uses in his descriptions and dialogues, and how that shapes our view of Kino and his level of responsibility. It is important to emphasize that students can only ask or answer questions that are based on the text—this is our evidence. We cannot extrapolate or imagine much beyond the words on the page. Questions must be focused squarely on the text although answers, if they involve thoughts or emotions, have a bit more leeway.

Defense lawyers and defense witness will likely emphasize the ways in which Kino sought to protect and nurture Coyotito. He rushed to his son's aid when threatened by a scorpion and even risked getting bit himself. He wanted to use the wealth from the pearl not for his own luxuries but rather to provide an education for his son. He risked his own life to attack the trackers, even though the unsuccessful attempt led to Coyotito's death.

The prosecution, meanwhile, will probably concentrate on the ways in which Kino's greed and his refusal to rid himself of the pearl put the entire family in danger. The areas of the text in which Juana pleads for him to eliminate the pearl from their lives are telling. He refuses and uses his "manliness" and "pride" as excuses.

A few key passages in the book illuminate how the prosecution and defense might build their cases. Let's start with the moment, on pages 5–6 (in the 1992 Penguin edition), when Kino attempts to save Coyotito from a scorpion. The defense has called up his wife, Juana, to testify since she was there. The defense sets the scene with questions like "Where were you on the day of the scorpion attack?" and "Who else was there?" After that, the lawyer could develop a series of open-ended questions such as:

- Where was the scorpion?
- What did Kino do when you both saw the scorpion approach Coyotito?
- What did he do with his hand?
- What happened next?
- What made the scorpion fall onto Coyotito?
- What did he do when he had the scorpion in his hand?

After the defense questioning, the prosecution comes up to build a case, based on a careful reading of the text and close-ended cross-examination questions, that tries to show that Kino didn't do enough to save Coyotito.

- Kino stood perfectly still at first while the scorpion was above Coyotito, right?
- He lost precious time doing that, didn't he?
- And isn't it true that at a moment when speed was necessary, his hand moved very slowly?
- Kino's role as a father is to protect his son, right?
- He was there, at Coyotito's side, when a scorpion bit his son and brought him to death's door?
- So, he didn't protect him then?

Another example with Juana as the witness can also show how close-reading of the language can allow students to develop legal questions that reveal a deeper understanding of the characters, their motivations, and their choices. On pages 55–7, Kino senses a danger outside, perhaps someone lurking to steal the pearl, and he exits the house with his knife. Juana rushes out after she hears a blow and finds Kino on the ground, bleeding. At that point, they have a discussion about the pearl in which Juana declares that it is evil and that they should rid themselves of the curse. Kino refuses and exerts his masculine authority to end the discussion.

Here, the prosecution has called Juana as a possibly hostile witness and will try to lay out the story with direct-examination questions, such as these:

- Where were you on the night right after you and Kino failed to sell the pearl?
- Where was Kino?
- After Kino stood up, where did he go?
- What did he have with him?
- What did you feel at that moment?
- Why did you feel that emotion?
- What happened next?
- What did you hear?
- What did you do then?
- Who did you see?
- What was Kino's condition?
- What did you sense?
- What did you do next?
- What did you do to help Kino?

Those questions have set the scene, but now we get to the crux of the prosecution's point, which is that Juana cared about the safety of the family but Kino did not:

- What did you say to Kino about the pearl?
- Why did you say that?
- What did you suggest that you should do with the pearl?
- Why?
- What did you say about the pearl?
- What did you mean by that?
- What did Kino say in response?
- What did he do in response?
- What did he fail to do?

At that point, the prosecution has laid out a strong case that they knew about the dangers that the pearl was bringing into their lives but that, despite Juana's warnings, Kino had taken the authoritarian position that they must not get rid of it. If child neglect includes "a failure to act" to prevent harm to a child, then they have laid a foundation for a guilty verdict. Equally important, from an English perspective, the students have used a close-reading of language like "evil" and "destroy" to develop an evaluation of the character and his choices.

The defense's case, in its cross-examination of Juana, is tough. The lawyers may choose to attack Juana for doing nothing and thereby diminish her credibility, or they may choose to offer a different interpretation of the event, or they may choose to illuminate what Kino did not do to Coyotito.

For example, they may try to show that Kino left the house to protect Coyotito:

- Kino left the house with a knife, right?
- He had already risked his life to protect his son from the scorpion, correct?
- Isn't it true that he put himself in danger when he left the house?
- He wasn't just trying to protect himself, he was trying to protect his son, right?
- Kino was a strong man, wasn't he?
- He was powerfully built?
- He was the type who could protect his son, wasn't he?
- He was fierce and determined, isn't that true?
- He was willing to go over the sea and mountains to sell the pearl?
- He was willing to do anything then to sell the pearl, right?
- And he wanted to do that to provide an education for his son?

Alternatively, they might emphasize what was not taking place to show that there is not enough evidence that Kino directly harmed his son.

- Kino never hit his son, right?
- Did you ever hear Kino yell at his son?
- Kino never left his son without someone to care for him, did he?
- Kino never suggested that you should put your son in danger, right?

Project Description for Students

Background: John Steinbeck ended his book *The Pearl* with Kino and Juana at the oceanside, disposing of the pearl and mourning their son's death. What happens afterwards? The town's jealousy is not gone. Imagine that rumors begin to spread that Kino is responsible for Coyotito's death. They left with their baby and returned with his corpse. What took place? Was Kino's negligence to blame for his son's death? Imagine that the rumors spread and Kino is arrested and brought into a courtroom to face formal charges. In each of your roles, you need to use close-reading of the language of the text to find out the "truth."

Our Question: Is Kino guilty of Child Abuse and Child Neglect?
The Indictment (Charge):
Count One: Based on his choices and failure to act in ways that would ensure the safety of his child, Kino is guilty of Child Abuse and Child Neglect.
The Federal Child Abuse Prevention and Treatment Act (CAPTA) (42 U.S.C.A. § 5106g), as amended by the CAPTA Reauthorization Act of 2010, defines child abuse and neglect as, at minimum:[2]

- "Any recent act or failure to act on the part of a parent or caretaker which results in death, serious physical or emotional harm, sexual abuse or exploitation"; or
- "An act or failure to act which presents an imminent risk of serious harm."

What Do You Need to Do?

1. Read sources carefully.
2. Annotate sources to identify evidence that supports your case.
3. Write 5–10 questions for the trial or prepare your answers as a defendant.

Stipulated Facts: Kino's Case

These facts are agreed upon by both parties:

1. Kino discovered, in the ocean, an extremely valuable pearl.
2. Kino and his wife Juana left town with the baby boy, Coyotito, and returned with him dead in her arms.

The Pearl: The Prosecution's Case

Witness Name	Role	Student	Page #s and Topic
Juana #1	Juana #1 Prosecutor (Direct) Defense (Cross)	__________ __________ __________	37–40 (the attack)
Pearl Seller	Pearl Seller Prosecutor (Direct) Defense (Cross)	__________ __________ __________	48–53 (Kino's attempt to sell the pearl)
Juana #2	Juana #2 Prosecutor (Direct) Defense (Cross)	__________ __________ __________	55–63 (a second attack)
Prosecution Opening Statement			
Prosecution Closing Statement			

The Pearl: The Defense's Case

Witness Name	Role	Student	Page #s and Topic
Juana #3	Juana #3 Defense (Direct) Prosecution (Cross)	__________ __________ __________	4–6 (the scorpion's attack)
Doctor's Servant	Doctor's Servant Defense (Direct) Prosecution (Cross)	__________ __________ __________	9–12 (Kino and Juana's attempt to get help)
Juan Thomas	Juan Thomas Defense (Direct) Prosecution (Cross)	__________ __________ __________	24–26 (Kino's dream for the pearl)
Kino	Kino Defense (Direct) Prosecution (Cross)	__________ __________ __________	The entire book
Prosecution Opening Statement			
Prosecution Closing Statement			

Notes

1. Steinbeck, J. (1992). *The Pearl.* New York: Penguin Books.
2. www.childwelfare.gov/topics/can/defining/federal/

Conclusion

The courtroom is often the setting for compelling drama in popular American literature and film, whether the behind-the-scenes dealings of *Twelve Angry Men*, the suspense of John Grisham's *The Firm*, or the sleazy dealings of *The Lincoln Lawyer*. While we know that the real-life dealings of most lawyers are far more tedious, the exaggerated tensions in those stories reflect a true drama at the heart of the law: the pursuit of justice.

Two personal stories, among many, stick out in my mind about the power of the courtroom. One of my friends once told me about how she became an attorney. She had been "unfortunate" enough to be chosen for a jury. She was, at first, reluctant to lose her time there but as she watched the case unfold before her she became "taken" by what she saw. Soon after, she chose to enter law school and now works as a labor attorney. The other involves a class trip to a United States Federal Court in Manhattan, which my colleague Andy Snyder had organized, to watch the sentencing of a man convicted as an accomplice to robbery. It was his first offense. He had been threatened and coerced into joining the crime. He seemed genuinely repentant and we had read his confession. Now we would learn the consequence. We sat there alongside the defendant's family as the judge cleared his throat to announce the sentence. We realized that this man's future was in the hands of this judge, whose view of justice would decide the defendant's fate. There was a sigh of relief as the judge announced that the defendant would not be sent to prison but would instead pay back the stolen money and complete community service. The defendant's mother then stood up to emotionally thank the judge.

The historical trials like those of Julius Streicher and Galileo, and literary ones such as those we could create about characters like Kino are just as dramatic. Moreover, they are events that help define our sense of justice. Why not immerse our students in a learning activity that brings up wellsprings of emotion and excitement? And when we begin to delve not only into the intricacies of a particular case but also its implications for the concept of "justice," then we are engaging in a deep philosophical and ethical conversation that has its roots in Hammurabi, Deuteronomy, Confucius, and Aristotle. We become part of that chain of thinkers who question what is "right," what is "just," and how we order a society in which we have some hope of achieving those lofty goals.

At my school, Harvest Collegiate, our work is embodied in our slogan: "Every student is an intellectual." To accomplish this, we engage our students in high-level academic work like mock trials. Now, I'm certain we don't want every student to become a lawyer. When we do these projects, however, we can be sure that students are developing the type of intellectual curiosity, ability to close-read texts, and habits of wonder that will allow them to become more capable members of our community and more rigorous critics of our society.